Maxims, Minims,
Thoughts, Essayettes
and Mini-Descriptions

BY THE SAME AUTHOR

Token and Trace
Metamorphosed from the Adjacent Cold
Leavetakings
Sleeping It Off
Cold's Determinations
Past Futures: Collected Poems *

*published by Shearsman Books

Clive Faust

Maxims, Minims
Thoughts, Essayettes and Mini-Descriptions

Shearsman Books

First published in the United Kingdom in 2018 by
Shearsman Books
50 Westons Hill Drive
Emersons Green
BRISTOL
BS16 7DF

Shearsman Books Ltd Registered Office
30–31 St. James Place, Mangotsfield, Bristol BS16 9JB
(this address not for correspondence)

www.shearsman.com

ISBN 978-1-84861-605-9

Contents

Acknowledgments

Such a book as this is inevitably a group activity, and I have had many friends involved in the production, promotion and resisting of its ideas, but also many friends, often the same ones, whom I've asked for advice about particular maxims, at whatever stage in their making I or they needed counselling.

There are also books from the past which I have burgled or pilfered from for lines phrases or ideas galore which I can partly lay to rest by overtly positioning them here in the setting of some of my maxims. But also, language and ideas don't shoot up in an individual space, and there is community at both the beginning and end of them.

About half the time I've made no attribution where an earlier author and one of his phrases is well known enough; other times I've used quotation marks, and times yet again have done that and made an attribution as well. But this is no formal work of scholarship, so I have not referred to specific pages, nor editions, nor even particular books. That is not because I am not indebted to, say, Wordsworth, for the phrasing, however I've twisted it, of the title to the 'Immortality Ode', but because these things are truly in the public domain, and deserve their own immortality, unhindered by my obscurity. Nevertheless I have usually attempted to note the sources, if not in full academic detail.

The friends I have received advice and encouragement and even promotion from include John Phillips and David Miller in England, Jan Bender in the U.S., Roger Sworder, Kris Hemensley, Michael Hallpike, Maurice Nestor and Dietrich Faust back here at home; and four female friends, also here, often with real insight and different (from male) slants on the type of social maxim La Rochefoucauld was so expert at, and myself so far less expert at. Reminding me that La Roche too had women's perspectives from those French salons where he would test out his insights, and perhaps sometimes their own insights, on often welcoming but occasionally unwelcoming ladies.

Di Sewell is one of my informants here, but has also been my companion over the three years in making of this book, as well as many years before; while the other women—Sally Holmes, Ros Webster and Cheryl Russell—have added company to this ageing poet, as well as valuable reactions to his work. And then there was my mother, of indomitable will and independence, but very adroit with people, who gave me many of the insights which went into the book, and many useful puzzles which are with me still. And, in all of this company, Harold Stewart, my main "friend in the Dharma", from the past.

The authors that preceded my work are too numerous to mention, though La Rochefoucauld, Guicciardini and the Ecclesiastes scribe have a special place, while Sinyavsky, Samuel Johnson and perhaps Ambrose Bierce are underrated in this genre. I'd be glad to be thought of as a minor member of their company.

Finally I need to make special mention of Cid Corman. So many of these maxims arose in a long dialogue, sometimes argument with him, over the epistolary years, that he should be known, probably, as co-author or collaborator and jousting partner; and I hail and farewell him yet again, seven years after his death, for his role in this work, which he living had no direct knowledge of—though neither then did I—as well as for so much else I owe him.

Before signing off, I will make the regular disclaimer. Except where I have used the name, or the initials, none of the incidents mentioned should be attributed to anyone, nor any of the quotations. The work, in that regard, is fictional, as indeed probably is the author. And how could this be otherwise, with whoever-this-might-be bearing such a name.

Cited: William Bronk, *Life Supports*; La Rochefoucauld, *Maxims* (Penguin translation); Walter Benjamin, *Illuminations* (I think); E. Conze, Buddhist Wisdom Books; Paul Celan, *Selected Poems* (Penguin translation); F. Guicciardini, *Maxims of a Renaissance Statesman* ("Ricordi"); C. Brancusi, *Aphorisms*; D.H. Lawrence (letters I think); D.T. Suzuki, *The Essence of Buddhism*; Cid Corman (letters); John Phillips (letters); David Miller, *The Waters of Marah* (and letters); Jan Bender (letters).

And acknowledgments to *Shearsman*, edited by Tony Frazer, *Connor Court Quarterly* edited by Brian Coman, and Kris Hemensley's online magazine, where some of these maxims first appeared.

Note: I have included later interpolations for a better blend. They are marked with *int.* for "interpolation" after the number, which is the same as that of the preceding maxim. There is no necessary relation to that preceding maxim.

Note 2. Many of these maxims come from earlier times and I have not updated them.

CHAPTER 1

1. It's funny how we sometimes slip into our past almost as if it were unfinished business.

2. I travelled across the Australian desert for a couple of days by train. A lot of rocks and some sparse bushes, but flat beyond belief and relief maps—for hundreds and hundreds of miles. Windless, when I saw it—and that was spooky. Space that looked like it had been waiting for something to happen, or not to happen—it didn't matter much which—for tens of thousands of years. I don't know, really, what we've ever been doing here.

3. Time stops still for a minute. For how long?

4. We attempt to avoid criticism from others by the strategy of criticizing ourselves.

5. "All truth—and real living is the only truth—has in it the elements of battle and repudiation." (Lawrence) So it rages back and forth—with not even an armistice? Let alone the distancing that you get on mountain peaks, looking down onto a small clear world, or in valleys looking up at the peaks?

6. The night sky, deep blue—with minutiae of light. Older galaxy patterns re-emerging.

7. Honesty and dishonesty are not always surface characteristics, nor remaining consistent through the whole of a person's character. People can have layers of honesty and dishonesty alternating to the depths of their being, with the base frequently slipping in and out of both honesty and dishonesty.

8. Walking out along a wooden jetty, on the lip of the ocean. One or two people fishing off the sides. Sounds blown away by the wind, so. But the sound of the wind itself, and a seagull call, or a pecking order squawk. And you need to shout to be heard a yard off, in the teeth of it.

(Along the Altona pier, near the house of Cheryl Russell, a friend.)

9. Whenever they concoct a new antibiotic for golden staph, the bacteria evolve into strains resistant to it. The micro-organisms are not stupid.

10. The turn of events—sometimes so slack as to be hardly drawing a breath.

11. Diagnosed with emphysema. Quite a shock to get the message; and, along with the advent of my next decade, has made me feel more temporary—the end within a gasp or two, so to speak.

12. We've had intimations of mortality from early childhood. But not the clinical discussions we will engage in later, as we stumble up closer to the event.

13. Losses of people. I don't really know how to cope. Oddly enough, the ordinary consolation that it is inevitable and universal, is more desolation than consolation for me: the idea of *so* much absence, and the dwindling in meaning of any one particular absence in the light/dark of that thought, of that *truth* in fact, is pretty much unbearable. I think how little now deaths of a hundred years ago mean, or fifty, or from one's earlier life, and how blasé was one's own attitude to the death of grandparents, as being inevitable with such old people. And it was—but...

14. It took a long time—seven years in fact—until my brother's death became past tense, historical. And now the gap is as great as to the Pharaohs or the time of the Mughal tombs.

15. The kid skidding down on the water slide nearly drowning himself, immediately springing up rejoicing in the spray, then attempting to mount back up on the slide against the slither and gush of the water.

16. He had avoided the occasions-of-sin in front of him with a sidestep he'd learnt, unaware that the occasions-of-sin behind him had accustomed themselves to his gait, and were stalking him stealthily from the rear.

17. The power, in love, lies with the one that wants the other one less; and it can swing when this particular pendulum swings, too.

18. Why is it that men dressing up as women seem to be funny, even ridiculous, while women dressing up as men seem stylish and strong? Is it just because women, by and large, dress up better than men? Or is it because women contain the whole of life, including men, whereas men are limited to the simply masculine, and are lost outside of it?

19. Surprising how easy it is, normally, to tell whether two people are sleeping together. It's as if they still carried each other's body warmth around with them from their bed, and had just separated themselves. Whatever, there's a physical ease in their relationship which is not present while the matter is not yet undecided.

20. "Everywhere I turn, there is the Face of God" as the Hadith puts it. It has its problems of course: you turn to Auschwitz, and there is the Face of God?

21. And *real* materialists, like Hume, who deny the supernatural, will often pull some very unlikely deity out of the hat—like the "invisible hand of the market" he invoked for his friend Adam Smith. A lot of obeisance to that Deity round the bourse cathedrals of the world.

22. As La Roche says, we assume that we will live for ever—though we "know" rationally we won't. And there is a certain level of awareness, which seems physically situated in us, that is immortal, and is neither an aged man, a youth, a "mature" adult, nor a child. No doubt it dies when we do, but it is easy to imagine it being unaffected even by that.

23. Should you interrupt your journey to get the car off the road, and halt for a tea break and an extended nap—or have a short refreshing death? Then get your car back on the road—if you can find it.

24. I've read that, at the Irish wakes, friends would have the corpse sitting fully dressed at the table in their company, with a mug of porter in front of him and converse with him as if he were still alive. All of it's whistling in the wind, but that's not a bad tune to whistle.

25. Ringing up the dead. I wonder if there'd be an answering service and if they'd get back to you?

26. The wail of the ambulance siren eddied on the wind.

27. Feeling well today. The body back into forgotten rhythms.

28. You've got to go out and get understanding for yourself—even if it's been there from time immemorial. It's not going to just hand itself over to you. And you're not going to be able to read about it in a book, for it will be in an indecipherable foreign language—that you know already.

29. Can Enlightenment be confused with endarkenment? And the mystery is whether, in the subfusc, you have basically the light or the dark?

30. As for "Eternity", timelessness rather than endless time was what people had in mind. Does "I saw eternity the other night" raise the question: and how long did you see it? For the instant of a lightning flash? Or in Vaughan's case, a sinking into the timelessness of the stars.

31. Some excuse for us oldies being settled in the past—after all we've got little enough energy to re-go through the processes of time. But what's the excuse for youngsters being settled in this present-turning-past? After all, the present lasts no time at all, and they've got the energy, and they're not stuck in a past past like we are. They should be looking to see what's to come, and *doing* it—so it can eventuate.

31 *int.* What would be my objective in life? To be stretched out as a leather strop for Occam's Razor.

32. We were in a holiday hotel on a cliff over the beach when a typhoon struck. All of the windows were smashed in by the gale, except a double-glazed one in the central lounge area, where the guests gathered. I saw palm trees bent horizontally, towering waves, and roofs ripped off buildings. And, against all our human feeling, I rejoiced.

33. While bushfires, wars and floods do bring out another, sometimes more noble, aspect to people, it is a mistake to think of this as a deeper aspect. The deeper aspects are the ones people display in the normal course of their lives.

34. "And we open our eyes and feel our way in the dark." (Bronk)

35. Life settles in like rain sometimes, and asks you questions like a leaky roof. It's too early yet, while it's raining, to check the roof—though you need to catch most of the drip-droppings in saucepans and buckets.

36.

37. The traditional image of the course of one human life is the Tao, the Path. It travels up and down, winds left and right, sometimes hairpin-bends back on itself, sometimes coincides with other routes for a while, then diverges. Where there's a mist on the way, or in the valleys, you often get re-sightings of the goal. But you don't know what in fact the goal is, nor the route, till you get there. And it's an interim goal anyway.

38. The apocatastasis, where everyone—and everything, down to "the last blade of grass" is enlightened. (Mind you, I don't have problems with blades of grass; it's *people* that're the problem.)

39. But Kali, "The Black", as Goddess of destruction and rebirth? Yes. With Winter pruning and then Spring (though rebirth occurs quietly in the middle of winter). A *great* myth that—and still consoling, at depth. In the shallows, though, it can be very painful. Whether it's ourselves that are to die/suffer, or our loved ones, and/or our world, and all we've known, in and around us.

40. You "reach out" (Cid Corman) the way the Chinese poets do, which is also a way of reaching in—without disturbing the surface tension of life by any ripple at all. And we pause there with you, above water, like a dragonfly resting on a leaf.

41. A little verse coming—a fickle trickle.

42. Still miss Frank Samperi and his letters. There'd be something about The Word from a living man or person. Not just that he's a "contemporary", but that the voice is coming to you now, without filter or echo from a sometime past, half-forgotten.

43. I said jocularly to a friend of mine years ago, "Do you believe in God, Ros?" Answer: "Well, it depends on the weather."

44. Seeking truth is more like a hunt—except that the quarry meta-morphoses from fox to amphibian on the bank to escape with a splash, as you're about to move in for the kill.

45. Contradictory curses—as when you curse the awkwardness involved in having a piss or shit. Do you *really* want to be unable to urinate or defecate? A really tricky—God would relieve you of the necessity and of the opportunity—to grant you both your constipation and your strangury.

46. I didn't know that Phil Whalen had lived next door to Cid in Kyoto, nor about the regular meetings in San Francisco when young. "…and we used to solve the world's problems together." Yes, I know that scene, and it's very attractive. Wouldn't particularly want to re-hear the conversation (in my case, with Ian Watson, say) all these years later; but that's mainly so those two young men could stay free of second thoughts, and continue being young. Besides, part of the correction would be to the *hope* they had; and I don't like snuffing out hope—even past hope.

47.

48. Literature, when I was young, would cancel out time, making me a contemporary, at depth, with Villon, Donne and Tolstoy. But now I am all too aware of the ages' receding pasts, and any "direct communication" with them is as through a vortex.

49. (*add.*) The "Splash" of Basho's frog still seems here/now, though. (Corman translation)

50. You've had a dry period for poetry, but suddenly the flood. As the words surge into you, you're interrupted by a visit from a friend not seen for a decade, who's never visited you before; or find yourself answering a once-in-a-lifetime telephone call. It's like summoning up the spirits— and their mood is distinctly mischievous.

51. "Brooding about my stupidity…" (J. Ph) I know that one from the inside. But it's not one's *relative* stupidity, is it? (though confusable with that), but one's *absolute* stupidity, *viz* no omniscience. And one defers not to relative non-stupidity, but only to absolute non-stupidity as the measure.

52. 10.30 a.m. And still a white touch of frost rime upon grass and bare trees, like traces of blossom.

53. Your queries (Jan Bender) about Nothing have awoken me from my dogmatic slumber. I'll have to start and stop and restart this cogitation—like one of the old cars with a crank—or the monoplanes and biplanes, that needed their propellers swung hard, then reswung, till they'd coughed into action.

54. The shock of opposites—like ice cream instantaneously wrapped in hot batter you've sunk your teeth into.

55. Not only does our body have a natural lifespan—if sometimes stopping a stage or two short of it—but our understanding has a natural lifespan too, managing two or three eras of cultural change in a lifetime, but giving up on any further adjustments to it after that.

56. The image the rationalist has for death is that of turning off an electric light bulb at a switch, perhaps with a dimmer.

57. Because the past cannot change, it seems to us anachronously that it never *had* been able to change.

58. I consistently see people, in unguarded moments, having insights, premonitions, empathies, discernments that they theoretically don't believe in. And their spiritual and mental poverty, with starvation in unbelief, undernourishes them in time, just as physical poverty does. Not that they are to blame for that, as they've been educated to ignore such insights and accept their poverty as inevitable in the matter-of-fact and spiritless order of things.

59. Alone, Twelve o'Clock, New Year's Eve, so I recalled my friends—and had our Auld Lang Syne with the dead.

60. That we think them of little ultimate value does not mean to say that we should ignore the formalities of the present, its customs and beliefs. A deep politeness to present understanding, and an acquiescence in their rituals is required as our social duty. But we must not confuse these with expression of the truth *tout court. That* is something which is our deeper

duty to find. But it is very confusing to both of our purposes that the political powers-that-be spend much of their time attempting to stage-manage these rituals, packing them with assumptions and readings that block access to truth, and suit their own very devious ends.

61. He was the soul and wit of a party he didn't want to be at. Not that he didn't begin to enjoy the role, partly as a perverse comment on the party itself and on his success in the comedy opportunity it'd presented to him.

62. We still need our Ash Wednesday, our day of fasting, after continuous Mardi Gras, to give us peace, and help us recuperate, so that, with systems cleansed, we can recontinue both the festivals and the indulgence.

63. The "common understanding" has a regimen of quarantine, Customs and border security—"to keep us all safe".

64. Wave on wave of birds' chirruping—like rustlings in tune.

65. Cliffs are dangerous places—but don't seem so in company, when the communal sense drifts a warm psycho-social haze over any danger near the precipice.

66. At issue is whether the social compromise of morality should be superseded, at depth, by more absolute standards—standards of the social outcaste. To say I'm in two minds about this is an understatement—I'm in *doubly* two minds. There is *some* correlation here with two basic types of art form—the visual and static versus the aural musical mobile and temporal. The absolute, as with the outcastes, does not tolerate the weight of settled conditions, and needs its temporal realities to be in motion and transition. Whereas the social relative needs its forms to be consistent, and is less concerned about any transcendent reality behind the forms.

So, one of them, the relative, will have no reality behind its forms, while the other, the absolute, has no way of manifesting itself. Leaving a real quandary for the artist, whose accomplished work will be either detailed and shallow, or profound and amorphous—except for the very few cases in which these will be juxtaposed into miracle.

67. A sort of Blind Man's Bluff you play with yourself—or with one or other of your many selves; and it's difficult to know where any of them would be hiding, and which one, if any, is doing the searching.

68. Autumn. Oak leaves fallen across path—like brown lizard tracks.

69. It's like spitting in the wind. "My taste was me."

70. "Where is anywhere? We make maps and let maps make us." (Corman) I like maps, contour ones, an inch to the mile. Some variety, and a relief from words. Or those Elizabethan maps, with whales blowing spouts in the corners as they do in the oceans.

71. The New Year's Eve party continued as if twelve had never struck—though closer to the intercalary time of skinny dipping and sex.

72. Cures calling up new viruses, retro-viruses, infra-viruses. Nature's imagination and intellect is at least the equivalent of ours—and it's not up itself, either.

73. Doggie serial-barking next door: "I'll just keep persisting till one of you gives me a further excuse to continue my barking".

74. I've seen very few men gabble baby talk at babies, gathering around prams, while the best of the women *talk* to them, not nod goo-goos with idiot smiles.

75. Summer, blinds down, sweatings through the day.

76. Vegetarian meals in Japanese Buddhist temples, where they cut the vegetables to look like leaves and flowers in artistic arrangements—such as at Barry Gazzard's wedding. What followed seemed a much more dainty activity than just eating.

77. There's somebody else's car on the back lawn, so I can't get the "grass" mown. And the weeds are summoning their mates. And wistaria's climbing along the back fence after taking over the side fence; and pumpkin creepers too, over the fence and across the lawn. I'm being invaded! Let's hope the empire sets up a sufficiently efficient administration to get this place reorganised.

78. Ross River fever and AIDS. Not the only diseases that've leapt from animals to humans over the last few decades. Pretty obvious reason: the

animal hosts they used to cohabit with are being exterminated, and the viruses or retro-viruses need a new life partner. Good to know we're still of some use.

79. A photograph of Cid and myself at Ninnaji in front of cherry blossoms and a pagoda. All of us in time, but the pagoda in very long time indeed. And the cherry blossoms in an ever-recurring eternity. (Photograph taken by Di Sewell, my companion then and since.)

80. Yes, "The Theory of Poetry" is just an effort to pen the wild beast, and hand-feed it with genetically modified grain like a yardful of chooks or a shedful of battery hens.

81. Full yellow moon—a cloud ridge, faint line across it.

82. Some people live in the relative, some in the absolute. Many more get them thoroughly confused, and especially imagine their relative is indeed an absolute, with nothing relative about it.

82. *int.* In the long run, "You can't know anything" or "There's nothing to know" is just a variation on "I/We know it all".

83. Snow stretched over some cars like tarpaulins, others with clumsy heaps of it, as if tossed onto bonnets and boots and roofs.

84. You think of a crushing reply to that last point, but the meeting's over and you're descending to the ground floor in the lift. Surely you can re-convene the meeting to make your rebuttal—then call an immediate halt to proceedings? (Batted about with Morrie Nestor and Roger Sworder)

85. Extraordinary that people try to get clearer and clearer perspectives on the future by adducing yet more evidence. There is some weird idea that you can completely collect *all* of the evidence to accurately predict everything ahead. But even then, all of this evidence would be from the past not the future, and could give no definite proof of what would happen then. Nevertheless we believe that if we mortar in all the bricks we have now, we will already have erected the building that it is going to be then.

86. It's good to be back in harness again—clip-clopping along a winding road.

87. Your cynicism is not well earned. You picked it up off the street when it didn't belong to you, not bothering to check out its credentials, or your own.

88. How do you get certainty out of mere probability? You quantify probability into certainty—"at that degree of probability". And we know then, with some precision, how certain its probability is.

89. Like a rat clutched in hawk's talons in the rat's imagination.

90. The "dilemma" is particularly sharp in the case of Adam and Eve— They are driven from the Garden into mortality and time, so that they are outside of time when in the Garden. But *events* occur in the Garden, things happen there *in sequence*; and would not make sense, or the sense they do, if they had not occurred in that sequence. And you cannot have sequence out of time—without before and after and during. The Sacred Time they occur in is not time at all—so no events can happen in it. And at last we have a dilemma: what is it that can only be narrated in time, but is, for all that, outside of time?

91. Some people escape immorality with a refusal to be moral agents. Somebody else makes both the moral and immoral decisions.

92. The Triads—in symbolism. The Chinese Great Triad, T—Heaven, Earth and Man. Or a conceptual one—Thesis Antithesis Synthesis (or its earlier versions in Neoplatonism—as in E. Wind). Or the Christian Trinity. Or the Past Present and Future. With a medieval mind (which I sometimes have) all these would be necessarily reflective of each other.

92 *int*. Most of the time I am in dialogue with myself. Sometimes I am in dialogue with other people. In the religious vein, one places the dialogue in a receptacle—no doubt into what the Christians call "God", or the Buddhists call the "Dharmakaya".

93. Some suggestions for a new decalogue, a *Megadecalogue* (or as my friend, Michael Hallpike suggests: A Heckofadecalogue.)

The idea originally was to engrave a new set of Commandments accurately setting out the *de facto* moral rules, and rules of custom, of the day. I became, unfortunately, bored with the task, or was tired and grumpy, because the idea woke me from my sleep. So I have only the more ironic of the new laws to offer my reader.

i. Thou shalt lie only on very special occasions, so that then thou shalt be more readily believed. (Guicciardini)

ii. Thou shalt tell the children thou lovest them, else they might not be able to work it out.

iii. Remember when thy neighbour asketh thee for money, to give generously of thy time instead, and be *really* nice.

iv. It is socially important to seem to be a good person, but thou canst not fake being good, as people are very discerning in such matters, and thou shalt be found out. So thou needst then to *be* good, to successfully fake the *appearance* of being good. (Guicciardini)

v. Thou shalt convert inconvenient virtues into vices, and vices-versa.

vi. Thou shalt not be negative.

94. Doubt and belief are on the same see-saw, saw-see together, and each one raises the other in prospect and retrospect.

95. The replacement of old categories, and their subsequent elimination. "He died from malnutrition"—as if he were lacking Vitamin B6, not: "He starved to death". And "she died from severe hypothermia", not: "she froze to death". So the language which might have made us one with the people of the past becomes an anachronism—as does the past itself. And we're all alone here—in however brief a timespan.

96. Not too worried that "You're old enough to be her father". But, when about sixty, I realized I was still being attracted by women—and I was old enough to be their *grandfather*!

97. Why do happenings seem emptier with age? You've seen so many events roughly of this type, that no particular one of them is so very special.

98. Dropsy. The body turning into reservoirs of water. But not where it's needed—in the discs of the spine—a lack to have you shrinking down into little old men and women. Air: not in the lungs, but in the hair, abducting its colour, absorbing it, encroaching on it in grey, then pure white. While making its inroads into the bones, osteoporosis, slendering them, uncreating its gaps. And earth: pulling everything towards it in a physical not psychological gravity, slackening to the earth, deathbedded on its back, returning to earth, to scatter bone, re-unmade into the elements again it was mixed from. And the elemental fire—quenched, earthed, choked of air, flickering, snuffed into darkness. And the elements, separated, isolated, in no reunion, picked off one by one, untangled—no longer promiscuous with each other. And the dot at the centre of the sphere where everything has come from, and now everything returns— the Creator, the Destroyer. Of no magnitude, yet it contains all things that have been and all things that will become, overflowing from it, then being sucked back into it, from everything on through the One into the Nothing.

99. Is there some residual humanity still, when age has left all the fragrance of youth out in the open air for far too long a time?

100. Evening. Within the dark branch-coverings of the forest, still, patches of light blue sky.

101. Breathtaking intellectual arrogance by people of monumental con- formist stupidity is really the feature of the day. (It wasn't around like this when I was young—the "acceptance" then was a different matter.) You are meant now to have *exactly* the insights that everyone else is supposed to have—and to imagine yourself as an "individual" thinker for having them. They are bulk-manufacturing such Individual Thinkers.

102. Some people look at you as from the blind side of a two-way mirror.

103. With everything that remains in my memory, there's been a query involved. I have, in the depths, been mulling over it all through the years. When I *answer* the query, the adjacent material, the penumbra, tends to slip from my memory, leaving just the solution to the problem, and the evidence for that, still occupying it there.

104. The most successful method for repudiating criticism of oneself, or one's opinion, is to attack the credentials or the character of whoever's been making the criticism. It was once considered a fallacy, called "ad hominem", but now seems to be as acceptable as any valid argument.

105. I'm very resistant to "You know?" Normally "You know?" means "They know". And I'm not one of them. And I'm certainly not one of "us".

106. "Things are getting worse." "But people have always said that." "And if they hadn't always said that, would you then admit that their saying it now is some evidence it might be true? And would you dismiss persistent claims that things are getting better on the same grounds—that people have always said that?"

107. One predicts the probability of future events from past ones. But not only don't we have the evidence of future events themselves to predict from, we don't even have the future's understanding of what would then be considered relevant past events. So not only do we lack some data, we may also lack the method for assessing whatever data we have.

108. Cathedral. Ribbed vaults lifted up, carrying echoes of the shutting of a nave door.

109. We've turned "free" from a relational term—free from prison, free from pain—into an absolute—particularly as a noun with the "dom" at its back. It's one of our many words—like "individual" (not-divided)—that are basically negative, but that we strain to make positive, as if we needed something indisputably more substantial.

110. "It takes offbeat people to begin to listen like that now, and I'm not at all sure it will ever happen again." (Cid Corman) Yep—on both accounts. Mind you, the whole society is "offbeat" now—literally as well—with music that's been bulk-syncopated. So "offbeat" is really onbeat, if you get my drift-rhythms right, and everybody's dancing in unison to a reaction against the beat.

(I'm not sure if this socio-musical comment is still contemporary since the advent of the "techno-beat", where both action and reaction cancel each other out, and there is as much rhythm as in a military march to the bass drum—or maybe even less.) (Leopold Faust for the bracketed insight.)

111. "Community values" instigated by media campaigns also have their use-by-date. They become as unfashionable as commercial products advertised in another era—eventually becoming unsellable, then unprocurable.

112. With television you are rescued from time, and live outside life in a room without death. Through a window you see recurring events being repeated from many eras in a time that's always today, but never moves on as today would. There are signs there are people outside the glass, but nobody moves in from outside to be with you.

113. For all that, we often do have to live as if people's sense of our given conditions now, the way things are, were in fact unarguably the right one—as a sort of deep courtesy to the communal understanding of things.

114. "Therefore, Sariputra, in emptiness there is no form or feeling, nor perception, nor impulse, nor consciousness; no eye, ear, nose ... mind; no forms, sounds, smells, tastes, touchables or objects of mind... There is no ignorance, no extinction of ignorance... There is no decay and death, no extinction of decay and death. There is no suffering, no origination (so much for the Four Noble Truths), no stopping, no path. There is no cognition, no attainment and no non-attainment." (Conze: Buddhist Wisdom Books)

115. Can the Mahakaruna (the Universal Compassion) be applied to everyone, and to everything? And, if so, can *we* apply it? Who are we to do it? Are we anything more than the application itself? Or something less? And which would be better, for us to be something more, or something less—or to be the same as the Universal Compassion itself? And how on earth could we be that?

116. Extreme Unction, Confession—rescued for eternal salvation at the last minute, when you might have been damned for all eternity. You bet heavily on the last race—if you can lay your bets on—in an attempt to recover your losses. Then somebody tells you the race is already run.

117. A kookaburra laugh, not so derisive as its echo in the forest.

118. Old Fogy's the nice phrase for us, Old Fart's the nasty. (It's bracing to call oneself that—to one's own enantiomorphic face: "Hi, Tweedle!")

119. The Animal Soul, naked and vulnerable to the incursions of the Spirit.

120. In age you are treated as a walking ghost well before you die. And you see the world like one too, with its distant affairs of not much interest to you.

121. We have histories to rescue time, pre-histories to rescue before-time, And the time that's been rescued doesn't mean anything—means as little as the time not being rescued now. Would it have meant as little then as it's meant since? All we have is evidence from then/there, accumulating like autumn leaves and clogging up our gutters.

122. Remember everyone that's dead. All of those with whom you've come in contact. All of those with whom you've never come in contact. Everyone from before the time you were born. All of them.

Chapter 2

123. The changes that have occurred in places you return to, the demise of attitudes that once seemed "inevitable", show not so much how things change with time, but how transitory they always were. The fundamental truth is not that things change, but that they have hardly ever existed.

124. The Miroku Bosatsu at Koryuji again. Strange effect that broken back has, and the clumsy board they've placed there as a spinal substitute. And the embrace of the novice lover that broke the dreaming fingers under the chin of the future Buddha, speculating on the saving of worlds to come.

125. Is sentimental empathy always an empathy for oneself? And does this radiate more sympathy for the other person, or less?

126. To youth, all older people seem to be inhabiting their natural roles, and settled in them, while only youths themselves are still in flux, lacking being and an ontologically complete determination, but perhaps yet "free" in a way their settled elders no longer are.
  I'm not sure the gist of this maxim is still contemporary. Youths have learnt to look upon adults as transients like themselves—though without any sympathy for that.

127. The rain leaving darkly dampened sides to cracks in the pavement.

128. Neighbour backed into my parked car—so it had a prang without me in it. Is it still in shock?—with me in after-shock?

129. Friendship between the sexes? It has an edge to it—sex at a remove. Possible when it's been metaphorically but not literally bedded down. The irritations then are *almost* the same as they would be in any long-standing friendship. Woman manage it better than men—and mismanage it better too.

130. When St. Paul says "Not I, but Christ lives in me", is he talking of something that comes and goes, waxes and wanes? And if so, how unstable as a foundation is that?

131. "Corruption is basic to our kind, and become our only kindness." (C.C.) Quite a few things are basic to our kind; but what's happening now has been pre-planned, on a couple of false principles, and is exponentially doing our corruption for us.

131. *int.* There is pretentiousness in normal people as well as abnormal ones; though we can more easily fail to detect it, yet can more easily take its measure when we do.

132. Wind stirring around bushes, trees—flapping foliage open, with no particular interest.

133. Summer lolling in on heavy air. No storm yet—lightning's in the distance, branch lightnings flickering across sky, followed by rumble. Nerves jangled, resettled. Mudlarks calling. There's rain you'd think, but the thunder's far off still. Yet rain's visible at a distance—in a fringe of blurry cloud.

134. Dostoyevsky's sense that the whole universe is on the line, with the tension of a final decision to be made immediately, is in another galaxy from me now, with dark-years of space between us.

135. I used to talk a lot and listen a lot. Then I began to talk more so as not to have to listen so much. Now I talk less and—though going through the motions—hardly listen at all.

136. The west windows of Chartres have been up there on the Gothic wall for over eight hundred years now. Sustained glass?

137. A civilization can grow old, not having had anything but youthful experiences.

138. You shut the door on the person from Porlock and return to the poem, much as you might return to continue a dream. And sometimes you succeed, re-entering the dream or poem where you left off, following its clear but crazy logic.

139. In that *particular* matter—deaths of those close—religion's no consolation for me. And the idea that we might all float up into the sky to

a re-enactment of our domestic life down here below is unimaginable—and depressing. How many people that we know—and that other people know and that other people's people know—would be involved?—and going back over how many decades or centuries? Quite a crowd, even if we didn't have a touch of agoraphobia—and we would have.

139 *int.* "Simplicity is not an objective in art, but one achieves simplicity despite oneself by entering into the real sense of things." (Brancusi)

140. I love Beckett's beautiful, patient and misplaced politeness. Gentlemen of leisure, those tramps, but gentlemen for all that.

141. I've had a bronchitis bug for over two months, and am about to commence an umpteenth course of antibiotics on the counter-attack. They might not be affecting the BIOS of the bug, but they are certainly affecting the BIOS of the bug-bearer.

142. It's difficult to be spiritual while you're sick—to have "the peace that passeth understanding". It's better to have a robust young body free of pain, to enable it to get on with life, as you detach yourself tentatively from it.

143. In writing you need to cut to the good bits as with a gangrenous foot—till something in you's screaming in pain.

144. First frost. Moisture inside the windows.

144 *int.* He's going to be a father. He went farther than he thought.

145.

146. Never played at: "Buck, buck—How many fingers…?" And Hoppo-bumpo, though rough, was not as rough as Release—where you would barge in through a ringed wall of enemy bodies to "Release!" prisoners they'd captured earlier in the game. Most of such games incredibly old—from hundreds of years ago. Kids don't play them any more here. Just like that—after enduring intact outside of the adult world through generations and generations of children—gone for ever.

146 *int*. We count each clone as separate and "individual"—to be distinct yet identical with its progenitor.

146 *int*. In age, you habitually become a caricature of yourself, a helpless parody of your virtues and vices, attractions and repulsions—even your good features end up as ridiculous—your burning eyes a vacant glare, your tolerance a lack of interest, your shyness an aversion to people, your aquiline nose a beak.

146 *int*. The question is whether the aging character, with its ridiculous perversions of what you are, is a travesty of yourself, or the real you.

146 *int*. A good deal of beauty is just in being young itself, with its health, its hope and its unruffled skin, and the fact that its long-term grotesqueries, such as hair sprouting from the beauty spots, have not yet developed to bring smudge to the image.

147. One sign of the apprentice poet is that he finds himself following, sometimes unwittingly, the phrasing, the prosody, the rhetorical rhythms of some elder poet who has him in his spell. Often the copycat poet can do it very accurately—in the way that a good mimic can, or like a kid following adult intonations and emphases to give his remarks more weight than his small size and years would normally give gravitas to.

148. I can bear finalities only in theory; and am not so keen on them in practice.

149. The modern atheist has "beliefs" very like those held in apophatic or negative theology, based upon universal denial—"neti, neti" (not this, not this); but they (we) don't want to *believe* they have beliefs. Beliefs should be positive, they think—much in the way the Ordinary Christians would see belief. And they must not have such positive beliefs as the Christians do—and don't consider there is such a thing as a negative belief.

Yet I see these people not as being irreligious, but as having a bare religion that is clean of images, being in the old terminology, not iconodules but iconoclasts—and Truth (imageless and contentless) is in practice their God.

150. As for Pascal's Wager—nothing lost if you believe in God and there isn't One; but you're on a winner if you believe in God and there is one—we've all backed certain Winners that've never come home. And Lady Luck's got some very strange Tarot cards up her sleeve.

151. The dead spider clutching its abdomen in rigor mortis, hanging onto its web. Months later: same spider on its web, still clutching the abdomen in rigor mortis.

152. Victory in a verbal dispute isn't worth much. Always the defeated would've summoned further arguments given time. And you never convince someone, just because you've won an argument.

153. What *might*'ve happened is irrelevant. *This* is what's relevant—presuming we understand this right. And whether or not you've got to where you might have gotten to, calculating the consequences of events that never happened is pretty senseless conjecture. The idea that you can control or predict long-term outcomes—at least in the middle of the enterprise—is way off anything I've ever seen in life, let alone when your understanding's based upon non-events.

154. "The ordinary—to us—is extraordinary in fact. But we have learned to be bored." (Corman) Not *with* you there. We can only take on so much of the extraordinary—and it is very important to take that much on. But if we take it on without let, then we won't get into the rhythm of taking it on then leaving it—it would be like continuous music without rests, pauses or even cadences. But taking on the extraordinary when we are ready for it, and its time is ripe (and that's *its* time)—yes. You hear the well-timed ping as the ball hits the racket.

155. You know where pretty much everything is, in your private disorder; and the little lady comes in and tidies up your house or your room, concealing everything somewhere in the middle of her very neat piles. What's the opposite to "Voilà!"?

156. Some women particularly have readjustable memories … They can work on an event at depths unknown to themselves until it is ready to reappear transformed into something more benign to their characters. My mother—bless her soul—was able to enact this subterranean procedure

more than once with the same event, reliving a variety of different memories of it, as convenient—and never needing to lie in the process.

157. I don't go to funerals—been getting into practice for not going to my own.

158. Everything in continual change? But we do have *relative* stability of objects, lasting for some time as what they are, and as what we would call them—such as the church/cathedral of Chartres since about 1200, but relative *instability* of objects also—such as the clouds Polonius has to distinguish for Hamlet "mighty like a whale", presumably looking nothing like a whale immediately afterwards. Thus time itself, at least as we experience it, has speedings up and retardations, relatively, with transience. So that even transience doesn't move at a uniform pace—as our ticking clock allegedly does.

159. Loyalty to a relationship-on-humdrum can be more to the ideal itself than to the person, and will be sorely tempted if a vibrant living alternative erupts into the course of its life—that's if it *wants* a vibrant living alternative.

   Mind you, the humdrum that is likely to be disrupted is not so much your partner's as your own—and you might find that this particular humdrum is something you still really want, though you've already lost it.

160. I don't choose my women, I let my women choose me. Most of them have made a very bad choice (and blamed me for it) (correctly).

161. The baby crawling on elbows to keep its fists with the breadcrusts in off the carpet.

162. Why the deepest marital disputes are over "nothing". Any real matter of dispute must be taken seriously and objectively, imposing its own rationality on the debate, which acts as semi-impartial adjudicator. On the other hand, these "nothings" are entirely unreasonable, allowing you scope to be entirely unreasonable yourself, while at the same time, other matters, as deep as the chasm that exists between two separate people, will be goading your response from depths unknown to you.

163. They do have fire breaks here, in the bush; but, with strong winds, fires can jump several miles, and throw sparks and embers incredible distances—for "spot fires" or worse. Anyhow, by and large, the bush fires this year have burnt themselves out, not before they've burnt everything else out with them.

164. We can be so neurotic about the importance of an occasion that we will overload it to make it sink, before it's ever had time to float.

165. To have only one relationship is to show yourself what shifting sands she is and you are, caught in the eddies of your encircled cove. The fidelity, then, is in principle only, lest you move out on low tide to some other beach, with exactly the same ebbs and flows, high tides and low tides.

166. I am a Sagittarian and can't resist occasional gaffes. I usually stifle them now; but once in every eighteen months or so one will emerge like pink bubblegum, inflate itself, and pop all over my face, before I have time to suck it back in.

166 *int.* Don't make my complaints for me. I'm quite capable of making them for myself—and doing a much better job of it.

166 *int.* You've got about as much depth of intelligence as the head on a postage stamp.

167. After a hot day, a cool air flow just above the surfaces of heat.

168. "Animals only have cries…" Probably. But the dog pets my ladies have *do* learn some words when they bother to, and are particularly literate with tones of voice.

169. At least since the Romantic movement, but I suspect well before, all culture has been in reaction from the time preceding—either its strictness or its looseness/depravity, its inhumanity or its spinelessness/softness; and it might seem that the problem swings from side to side. But we can no longer react against Victorian prudery and hypocrisy as they were—such are, by now, historical phenomena. So the clever thing is to recreate these phenomena in the required image, and to continue the advancement,

the evolution, between well-defined alternatives, *both* of which are to be permitted by the powers-that-be as the only ones in our lives. As for the truly new alternatives, they might be forced upon such powers, but they will attempt to dress up the older alternatives in newer fashions, or newer fashions in antique dress, so each could pass for the other, while they still control things. And they have been remarkably successful at it. Think of the alleged continuing *rebelliousness* of the off-beat in rock music, and the equally alleged "daring" in clothing styles of newish bright colours, and designs cut close to the female genitalia and mammary glands—as they have been from time immemorial.

170. There's still bush out of town, near Bendigo. Lots of gum trees—very straggly, and not marshalled into ranks like the pines, but magnificent one-by-one—like the tall "Ghost gums". Not meant for people, this place—especially people like us.

171. People don't want to know about it—though they *do* know about it. They know precisely what they don't want to know about it.

172. The hammer used to nail up the silence.

173. When we say a person has a soul we are, at best, describing something adjectival about them, like some feature of their character, instead of indicating something nebular within them, which they have as a possession.

174. "X looks older than me now." Aged banshees look a bit older than just old. They were old before they were born—and still look like it never happened, but that it left its mark.

175. Dancing down a long ballroom floor hours before the ball—no other dancers on the floor yet.

176. Wind across under shed roof, whistling through rafters, joists and corrugated iron.

176 *int.* As for "meaning" you can't have certitude there, positive or negative. Life's no dictionary—to give you, when you look it up, a definition of the terms.

177. You think too quickly, and don't give yourself time to catch up.

178. Gold and red maple leaves shed by branches into lane at the back. Frost. Boots on. You crunch on over it.

179. "Blessed are the poor in spirit" should give the Fundamentalist Christians pause. They've got the spirit to be very rich indeed.

180. The logical gaps in "practical" contemporary thinking? Lots. But try this one. We have the problem of the understrata and of whole masses of "underachievers". Is this a problem? Well no, it's said, because any one of them can still make it through—in fact a small handful do. Fact—and proof! So *any* of them can make it through. So *all* of them can. Put like that, I hope, this looks as illogical as it is. But they're *very* satisfied with the validity of this argument.

181. Your first home ownership. Funny how settling in and a sense of finality and mortality go comfortably and uncomfortably together.

182. The mass slaughter of one's friends and relatives as the only living alternative to dying oneself. As another survivor said over the phone the other night: "Remember you are not alone." Well it feels like that, and it feels like they were too.

183. Woman are better at the social context of death than men, just as they are by and large at any social context. But death, notoriously, reaches beyond all social contexts, and there women are just as much outcasts as men are.

184. "You should at least have hope." Hope-only is a species of despair. Hoping-against-all-hope is to admit no grounds for hope, and no possibility of it. You are to hope *against* whatever evidence there is, meanwhile conceding that such hope is completely irrational.

185. The monk's scuff-shuffling in loose slippers across a temple's verandah floor.

186. I have trouble with my roof and my stumps. But I have trouble with *ownership* too. A sort of campsite, where we are in this world. Places

are only on loan, and will be reoccupied as soon as we move out—in a removalist van, an ambulance, or the pine box with the neatly fitting lid. So it doesn't matter then whether we've rented it or owned it. And people will redecorate the house to get rid of all traces of anyone who had ever been living there.

187. We think of despair as frozen, but it is more often in motion; and any immobility then is just a phase in its slow mobility.

188. After enduring the imposition of the spirit and the will for so many decades, the body finally takes over, making incessant demands, with the ageing spirit cowering beneath this new domination. "An old man's eagle mind" indeed, grounded, with broken wings, flapping scuttling across the earth and rocks.

189. The spread of neural alleyways in the blood, in anticipation and fear.

190. "Pray without ceasing"? Just keeping in touch.

191. There really is a sense that psychology, even when it gets things wrong, is clearing the ground—or analysing the material—to reach a *complete* understanding of the human mind or character. Whereas what *is* happening is that we are reconstructing our understanding of the human to conform to psychological concepts, and even, that we begin to trim our behaviour, and certainly our self-analyses, to the concepts and explanations of this analytical set. So that, eventually, the explanations, the analyses actually do become closer and closer to being true, as people's behaviour more and more closely conforms to them.

192. We're on parole from somewhere; and if we break certain unknown conditions of our parole, will be recommitted to whatever detention centre we've been released from.

193. "Hypocrisy is the tribute vice pays to virtue" (La Roche). Rather "lip service" than "tribute" I would have thought. Though it does give some acknowledgment to the particular principles it's flouting.

194. Anyone who thinks that time ticks along with the regularity of a metronome and an invariant pacing, will get his own life rhythms out of

kilter with the Allegro Vivace or the Andante Moderato of the whole of the rest of life.

195. I'm facing up to my regrets so I can refuse to have them.

196. Reflected light off the pool on the low ceiling of the verandah roof: wavelets in silent bumps.

197. They talk about the energy of youth—and it's true. But there is also a divine lassitude you have then stretching to infinity, that you never have again, all too aware, later, of the brevity of life, and the rapidity of its decades, and how little time will any longer become available to be squandered on such ecstasy.

198. Dining room fire just catching—a room laced with cold draughts.

199. The idea that money's a commodity is a very weird one indeed. You buy it and sell it along with pumpkins and tampons, and the price of money goes up and down like the price of tampons—though the price of pumpkins fluctuates with the price of money, while the price of money is unaffected by the price of pumpkins. But what do you buy and sell money with?

200. We wear artistic works out, or else cling to them as we do to our youth. And the next generation wants them out of the way like they want us out of the way. And we oldies, while we fume about it, tend to admit it's the best policy, and at times wouldn't mind getting rid of the passé art and the passé people, and joining the young so that we could have instead a nostalgic moment or two in a resurge of such energy.

201. God knows what weird signs are involved when men engage in a handshake. The strength of the grip is supposed to have some connection to the forthrightness of the character; but it's very much like stags locking horns.

202. Women don't usually shake hands with other women, but peck, kiss or hug. And offer men white gloves from very limp wrists.

203. There's a laughter that indicates how predictable such a turn of events would have been—usually evoked when nobody's in fact predicted it.

204. And I know how time stretches from their deaths, now. So, four days since Cid died, six years with my mother; eight with my brother. And I'm aware of them all—all receding. And how Cid's death *will* recede too, retreating further and further into the distance, more and more away from us.

205. Flowering wattle everywhere in late winter—with some of the visual fragility of cherry blossom.

206. I've been sympathetic to *very* different thoughts and *very* different approaches to life. But they don't just sit there together complacent with each other, without nit-picking, just as different sorts of folk don't. People dive into this pool you're going to get splashed—or drowned.

206 *int*. What they take from us in the future, if anything, will be *their* decision, not ours.

207. Seagulls floating on air, up down as if on water.

208. I'm ready to defrost memories of this insult any old time you like.

209. My trouble was, a friend explained, that I saw too much of what was happening with people and in people, and so was handling more evidence than I needed to. I think he was being overkind to me. But it's useful to know you can have *too much* evidence for an understanding.

210. One needs not only "to adapt oneself to the circumstances", but to the new era's rules of conduct, to pass an immigration test for the next period in one's life. True, you can sometimes live out in the backblocks where the rules change only slowly, but even there deportations will occur.

211. Layers of cages of hens in a truck, dropping feathers everywhere, rising up and down like a multi-deckered mattress over bumps.

212. Fogging up from distinction to indistinction.
Fogging up further from indistinction to extinction.

213. I'd reached full maturity by the age of thirty six, have been immaturating backwards to where I came from ever since.

214. Internally, the idea of maturity seems ludicrous. You know the same chaos is there, within and without, and that the ways of reading order into it are a sham, moving compulsively on and off the stage, generation after generation; and the only thing you have learnt is that you have learnt nothing.

215. "Start off with your conclusion, then 'reason' towards it."
"And what's wrong with that? It saves you some trouble."
"And it saves *them* some trouble, too."

216. The idea of the world being thoroughly clear of us—me particularly, but not just me (that, by itself, wouldn't make it sufficiently bare)—gives me the sort of contentment one has only at the solution of a purely logical puzzle—a deep satisfaction at the *finality* of it all.

217. Late sunlight off the water—prickly, with no heat.

218. People in agricultural societies saw themselves in the life cycle as like animals or vegetation, with birth growth decay and death coming along at the allotted times. We still see growth that way, but later work to understand ourselves as ageless "individuals", that decay and death should not be required to happen to—and that death comes to, when it does come, with the suddenness of a motor accident.

219. Blackberries hidden in prickles.

220. "To be nothing. Simply nothing. It's a frightening experience (though exhilarating too, I think). You have to let go of everything." (C.C.) Yep. Mind you, I can't think of an alternative to letting go of everything— that's if it doesn't let go of you first.

221. "I" am a circle whose circumference is everywhere, and whose centre is nowhere.

(Corollary to a proposition by Nicholas of Cusa)

222. We hanker after an earlier time because it seems more trouble-free than ours. But it's only that truly past problems have been resolved, buried or blown away over the ensuing years, while the ones that are still

with us from then are *our problems now*, rather than ones we imagine as disturbing a settled past.

223. I lift a wire gate, then scrape-shut it.

224. If you've got an opinion, throw your hat in the ring—it's only a paper hat.

225. "What does 'life' mean to you?—assuming it means anything." If you're talking about the word "life", a dictionary definition would do it. If you're talking about LIFE ITSELF, I'm not sure why you've put the quotation marks in. But an answer: *words* have meaning; some signs have meaning in a derivative sense; but Life Itself is neither meaningless nor meaningful. You can have a purpose in life, it's true, or two or three at different stages. And in this sense, life might have "meaning" for you. But Life Itself has no meaning, nor does it lack one. Neither of these qualifiers is applicable to Life Itself. To think of either of them as that is a category mistake—as if you could look up not just the words but Life Itself in a dictionary.

226. The concentric rings of silt left by a drying puddle.

227. Anybody who *never* thinks about those who're dead , and about the transitoriness of life, has got a sub-human depth to him that anyone still human among us would fail to understand.

228. Fundamental images? I see the whole thing as mobile hieroglyphics now, anyway (a hieroglyphics I often can't read), so the more salient symbols come in and out of the ranks with everything else. "Insane, mysterious" certainly—though I have the feeling we're just not clever/ intuitive enough to nose out what it's about, but get occasional whiffs. If we *do* get close to where it's been, it might well change its nature anyhow—it's not pegged out for our convenience like a drying skin.

229. The slow movement of the *Waldstein*—counter-rhythms searching and questioning, with false starts and false stops.
    (The collaboration of Dietrich Faust and Ronald Stewart)

229 *int.* Watercourse dripping past bracken lace, down banks onto the moss across rocks.

230. They pollarded the seven gum trees that'd been there for a hundred years, lopping off the tops and all the branches. Three weeks later tiny branches with new leaves had grown out of the residual ancient forks of what had seemed dead trunks—little clumps of it in nooks of the trees.

231. Romantic music makes a special connection with actual time from the empathetic feeling that is required for any linkage to it. With Mozart, on the verge of Romanticism, there is even a peculiar pain with such formal perfection edging its way into time.

232. I certainly don't see the spaces of "chi", and the brush strokes framing the spaces, as having meaning only in relation to us. *We're* lucky to have meaning in relation to it.

233. I'm more pessimistic than you. You believe everything's finished; I think we've some way to go.

234. The only one of the musicians you nominate—"Rubinstein, Perlman, Stern, etc." that I've heard live is Stern, on a warm night forty five years ago, concentratedly glued to his violin, sweating like a pig, playing the Sibelius. Except, of course, for "etc.", whom I've heard again and again, and forever beyond recall.

235. Light flickers on and off ruffled layers of leaves.

236. I aired that wish—about wanting to have another crack at life—in jest. Then thought that some sprightly demon might instantaneously take me up on it. Once is enough. Not too much; just enough. Besides, in a Buddhist mythology—their fairy tales—you'd end up in one of the *other* five worlds—as a "hungry ghost" for example, not in this place, to get it all right/wrong again, in exactly the same way. We've done our stint here—for whatever that was worth.

237. Rang Jan Bender to see if she was O.K. She was a bit confused when she answered the phone, as she presumed I was the man calling to fix her heater. Where there's smoke there's fire? Not apparently in the Vermont frosts.

238. Stained glass. Stone mullions down, stone transoms across—cutting through the light to radiated shadow.

239. He died young, she lived to a ripe old age. But there are no relativities in death; and when you're gone, all distinctions have been equalized and finalised.

240. By the age of forty—with a few years of practice—I'd learnt how to live the life of a thirty-year-old; but the time had passed, and my experience was now obsolete. And I started to realize that this would be true whatever new age group I was entering. So I began at last to comprehend the bewilderment on the faces of some old people, marooned not only in a new era they knew little about, but a new stage in their own lives they had no experience of. And that much of the experience they had accumulated over the years was now irrelevant to them.

241. Kids playing at the fruit and vegetable market—in and out and under stalls, bruised peaches and other fruit spread all over the area.

242. The night back home as a five year old after my tonsillectomy. Parents shifted my bed into their own bedroom; then later, in the middle of the night, after blowing my nose pretty incessantly, I woke up fully, when the electric light was switched on, to find my handkerchief bedsheets and pillowslip all soaked in blood. I'd been haemorrhaging—still was—and they rushed me into hospital just down the street, etc. Bit of a shock, so much blood there—and all *mine*.

243. A lot of your knowledge of people is knowledge of how to deal with people. It begins to relax and dissipate when you no longer have dealings with them, or when you are allowed to deal with them only in the restricted way the aged are—as no longer accepted competitors against them in the contests of life.

244. You're not immediately aware that you have grown old—as onlookers and acquaintances would be. You have to deduce it from the evidence.

245. (Finale) Something else, but I can't remember what.

CHAPTER 3

246. Comes a time in late childhood when the young lad knows it all, and has a complete and mature understanding of life, above his cowering juniors. Then puberty, and a shaking up of the hormonal glands, and the spectacular rise of Venus from the waves, and a new set of dilemmas not envisaged in the lad's premature maturity. And he becomes a little boy again, in adolescence's childhood.

247. We are all children, even the oldest of us: children who will never grow up.

248. People come in and out of our lives casually and accidentally, as if our train were late, and we had to ask a stranger if he knew whether they'd rescheduled it, or whether this one was still meant to be departing on time.

249. A lot more pain around than before and a lot less pleasure. And the two have got some deep connection with each other—the pleasure converting gradually into the pain.

250. I was wrestling devils and angels, without much ring-craft—they'd formed a very successful tag team against me.

251. The dismissive phrases, "that's it", "when it comes down to it", "let's get down to facts"—where the phrases have so much weight because they are brutalising reality, and one isn't allowed to nitpick about anything more complex that reality might be, but are bludgeoned into accepting "the obvious" that it is.

252. As a kid I slept one night in the corner of a room lit by a fire while the adults played cards—the two ages mixing together as uneasily as the firelight and the shadows, and myself drifting in and out of a dark but warm world of firelit unreality, mixing past and present as I do now.

253. Disregard the judgments and opinions of the past? It's not that what's been said before is irrelevant, it's rather that what we took for *granted* had been said before is irrelevant.

254. White breath-vapour drifting misting over areas of grey fog.

255. "Why does he hate you so much?" "I don't want to know. I see no reason for tip-toeing my way around the adjudication of my enemies as a method of understanding myself."

256. A small section of the congregation, or populace, will take the revered God or idea seriously, and ask "What is God?", "What is Freedom?", "How do I stand in relation to God or Freedom?" And maybe beat their heads against the wall to bludgeon the Truth in. But for most people going to Church is a social event—and you kneel when the Sanctuary bell rings, and stand to sing "Faith of our Fathers" after the "Ite missa est"—whatever—the faith of your fathers would have been.

257. Sunlight on the path, hot, direct, buffeting me as I emerge into it, creaking open a fly wire door.

258. During my working life, now finished, I could tell the time any hour of the day or night, within a couple of minutes of the actual time, and mostly to the minute. It was as if I had an internal clock, which I could consult in much the way you'd check with your wrist watch.

259. "Religion is the opium of the people"? *Conformity* is the opium of the people, both in its religious and irreligious strains; and never more so than when it has a deceptive air of older-style non-conformity about it to confuse everyone, including the alleged non-conformist himself. For it is *today's* conformities that they will be hankering to conform to, however long or short a duration "today" is going to be.

260. Mist in and around trees, dissolving not things but images of things.

261.

262. Sun through haze, shadow dappled from the trees, stretching diagonal across pavement—shadow crossing over under-shadow—double-dapple shifting in a slight wind to back again.

263. I knew he was very ill, yet his death, I felt, was impossible—which is how I usually feel about deaths in particular. In general, however, death's a necessity—and feels it.

264. Death-in-little and love are linked together; and orgasm is a tiny form of dying. And braving the shock a miniature test for braving both the death fear and the death wish.

265. Is life essentially dramatic? Or comic? Or do we have—as Bronk insists—no story, no history?

266. The barrister's job is to argue his client's case, not to seek for the truth, unless that suits his case. And he trains for the set of skills needed in debating tournaments and speech contests, where they nominate a subject of interest or of no interest to him—as the case may be—to argue for or against as directed.

In the process, he learns to transfer these skills and argue for himself as if he were a client, protecting whatever fortifications he happens to be standing in front of. It is similar in method to the salesman's task of promoting whatever goods he has in stock. The quality of the goods or of the stance is not an issue.

For the professional lawyer and salesman, these are their jobs—that's what they *ought* to be doing. But it would be intellectually perverted of *us* to forego the search for truth to find what specious arguments we might misshape for the·· purpose: to buttress the position we happen to have, and not examine it to find its fault lines and cracks, and estimate whether the structure is still stable.

And the idea of winning or losing as the only alternatives, and that someone can receive a final decision on these matters in this courtroom—with no double-jeopardy on either side—must explicitly inhibit any journey over the lengths and breadths of the globe to see the vastness of the world's problems, and some hitherto undreamt-of possibilities for their solution.

267. Sitting down in moonlight on sand under a tree shadow.

268. Men get interested in babies when they begin to crawl, walk, talk, and otherwise behave like human beings; not just loll there—like baby seals without flippers.

269. The devastation I've been feeling from the sense of universal obliteration is something new to me. Basically, before, I felt it good that all traces of me/us would begin to dissipate, then be swept clean away. I liked the

idea of the total hygiene of death, and of the *absolute* discontinuity. This other feeling is something new, something unexpected, and something I'm unpractised to cope with. It's never simply supplanted the earlier feeling though; just (sometimes) vies with it unexpectedly—but breathtakingly: that it would be dreadful/beautiful that no trace of us would ever be left at all.

270. A sportsman: "Life is not a dress rehearsal". And I had to wait till nearly seventy to have it confirmed? Can I audition for another role, preferably in an unsuccessful farce (like the present one)?

271. We don't want to forget those close to us when they die, but we do need to get on with our lives—and without them. So there is a terrible guilt about neglecting them, even though there's no longer any communication between us, nor any chance to bring them back into the course of our lives.

272. I was once a wages clerk, and would have my books all balanced of a Friday night at the end of the week, when one of the foremen would ring up with some labourer's overtime he'd forgotten to put on the pay sheets. I would include the overtime, then try to rebalance the books. But I never could, the second time round. And was "capable of" adding up a list of figures, pounds shillings and pence, from bottom to top, then top to bottom, and getting the same wrong answer each time. What extraordinary process goes on in your head to enable you to do something as tricky as that? We possess and are possessed by obscure skills and anti-skills beyond any everyday comprehension, that can juggle our lives like an acrobat or a clown, beyond our control but within their control, whether we want them there as our "abilities" or not.

273. The only thing no one minds being complained about is the weather. "Isn't it hot!" We don't respond with "You'd whinge about anything."

274. When earlier and unsuccessful types of human life—cultures, communities and occupations—have lapsed at last into silence, they disappear unheard, and then such options will be lost forever. A record of them, at depth, is poor substitute for the living reality, but better than no recollection of them at all.

275. "Many of our daily words are very vague and ambiguous." Like "very", "vague" and "ambiguous"? It depends on what standards you set up for them to fail to match. They give you vague thoughts very exactly. And "exactly" is not less vague, as a term, than "vague" is—or, really, "vague" is as exact a term as "exactly".

276. You know the Lewis Carroll story about the German cartographers who kept on making bigger and bigger scale maps so they could fit all the detail in? And finally they made maps a mile to the mile; but the farmers objected to them being spread out over the countryside, because they kept rain off the crops.

277. The modern approach to life is affected by advertising. We are trained to sell ourselves like commercial products, and "grow" these products to be sold in the marketplace. It is very different from any moral and life training we have had in the past, and a very different sense of what we are, and what we might be, that could have had such a training.

278. Don't tell me anything! I'm learning to forget things now, not in retrospect but in prospect.

279. If I understand it, there is a further stage after identification with the One-without-other: identification with the Nought. This phrase describes what happens in earlier stages, too, as "self-naughting", but its purpose then was to remove oneself as a distinguishable object, so that you could be identified with the One. What I am talking about is a later stage, and often associated with worship of wrathful forms of the Divine such as Skanda Karttikeya and Fudo Myo-o. At either of these two stages, "mortification" is the practice—the "dying to oneself"—but the latter cuts the "ground" from under one's feet.

281. At death, we often leave unfinished business, and unstarted business too.

282. The Christian Trinity is identified with the three phases of time, on the West fronts of the cathedrals—see Chartres for example. One enters the Church through the central of the three portals in which Christ represents the Father, and which is the instant Now. The right hand door shows Christ as human (plus the Virgin) and is the past and

the culmination of the House of David and all time that has preceded. The Left Hand door shows the Holy Spirit as Church as Future—enabled by the Ascension. It is arguably the same relationship to past present and future that one finds in the Taoist triad—though Christ standing in for the Father (we can only come to the Father through Christ) complicates things considerably, not *just* meaning: you can only come to the past through the present, or—you can only come to the immortal through death and the mortal.

283. A belief in "a Virgin Mary … equally silly." One of the reasons Catholic women always took to her: she didn't need bloody men. And the divine Kid was *all hers*.

284. As a couple of my women friends have pointed out subsequent to this, the Virgin Mary has become a role model for single Catholic mums, the Lady patroness saint of the solo woman's family.

285. Does the wind carry messages?

286. When the wind drops, does the silence carry messages?

287. I tend to see fundamental positions as something like aspects of the truth. (I'm not thinking of the hired gun, the lawyer, who argues from a fixed position that is non-negotiable.) But there are basic, almost temperamentally different, philosophical stances that—we would hope—will prove in the end to be complementary—such as the dependence on the stable and the certitude, compared/contrasted with the need for change, renewal, and the hitherto excluded.

Mind you, they are unlikely to live quietly with each other, and are likely to alternate in taking the dominant position, unless one totally overwhelms the other in the culture—and even then the other will seep through. In any particular culture, though, some human traits will be blocked from seeping through.

288. "Eden" is the place of the Platonic forms. You have only meanings there—as with words. So Adam and Eve are archetypal forms—using Jungian language—and not people. What happens when they are "driven from the garden" is the interesting part, at the junction point of time and timelessness—a puzzle to say the least. It's like asking: What happens

before time, and how long does it take to happen?—which *seems* like a proper question, slipping easily into interrogative form, but is as invalid as any answer to it would be.

288 *int*. Why do we move and live so slowly in age? Are we attempting to cheat death by advancing towards it more slowly, while it advances towards us more quickly?

288 *int*. We are accumulating the truth (?) And accumlating the falsity(?)

289. Half of the concept game we have with "Nothing" is because of its odd use as a noun or pronoun in circumstances where no thing is being referred to—as in "Nothing's missing"—where, if people took the word as a full substantive, they might ask "What *is* the nothing that's missing?" But the other half of "nothing" is in loss—the void where friends were, places we knew—and the rest (and the unrest). Just as important as any of the *words*, for me—and "sunyata" would be the most important single one—are certain images I have of it, such as 1. The sacred spaces in a Gothic cathedral or a Japanese temple. 2. The two-dimensional-plus spaces in Northern Sung landscape paintings (very important to me). 3. Certain geometrical figures—such as the "dot" at the centre of a circle, and the circle itself which is the expanded form of that "dot" (and likewise with the three-dimensional sphere), and 4. On a mountain peak, with the setting sun behind, looking over the valley below already being filled by a faint mist. Myself being "part of" these nothings doesn't, theoretically, fill me with dread. The point about "sunyata" is that *that* void is also a plenum. To say I have all this "clear" would be ridiculous. I'm not sure that I *want* it "clear". There are quite a few "coincidentiae oppositorum" in this ever-changing mix, match and unmatch, and you can only hold those together by admitting that they will never be under your full intellectual or intellectuo-somatic control.

290. The English in particular tend to lean the whole of their weight on the qualifying adjective, while the noun is mainly a post to hang this decoration on.

291. Baudelaire relates the deep ennui of the writer's task—the someone who is not within the local community, but moves anonymously (and without trade or caste) in the "Crowds" of the great modern city, that's

been, as-it-were custom-built for such an outsider. But now *nobody* is of a particular trade or caste, nor inhabitant of a particular locality. So the poet is no longer an outsider, as there's no inside for him to be an outsider from.

292. "I haven't been to The Muse* more than once or twice in the past thirty five years." (Corman) She's visited you though. Hope you've had o-mochi and o-cha laid out for her. Forgotten where *I* live, recently.

*A coffee shop that was a favourite haunt for poets in Kyoto.

293. We flick open our purpose like a paper fan, flick-fold it back between bamboo sticks of lacquered silence. Fasten it again against any inadvertent unfolding.

294. As for death, people keep putting it off, like writing a will, and only think of it when they have disturbing symptoms, or when somebody close dies, and death at last's at hand and unignorable. And even then, they will keep putting it off.

295. Headlights moving through fog within circular nimbuses.

296. Tired, tired. Attracted to the Big Sleep? The Little One I find difficult to obtain. The Big One I still have my doubts about.

297. All my friends, dead for so many years—even their ghosts are dying.

298. You see a spider, which also notices you spotting it. And the motionlessness is tense, visible—almost as visible as the scuttling-off would have been (though it's in you too). Similar to the silence of a person asked an awkward question about somebody else, when the silence falls audibly, and the answer is indicated unquestionably by the silence itself.

299. The ding-ting of bell birds in a slight mist.

300. The memory of times past exactly as they were. So that you could walk in and notice things you hadn't observed the first time round, yet they were still undisturbed, waiting there to be noticed.

301. Unity? Mathematically, I'd put "beyond good and evil" at nought rather than one. I know the One of Unity is "the One without other", nevertheless even that has a Dark Side of the Sun to it, and we stand under whatever it is like an unseen shadow.

(At the instigation of a prose poem, 'Messages', from *The Waters of Marah*, by my friend, David Miller—a fine and intricate work.)

302. "…be devious, as my mother always said." (John Phillips) Women are pretty skilled at being either devious or direct—as they choose, and as you don't choose, and as they choose you don't choose. It was very kind of his mother to get him up to speed on this. *My* mother believed I should be completely entangled in women's wiles, and that that was the correct thing for a man to do—to be undone.*

* There's a grain of truth in this, but mostly it's unfair to my mother.

303. It's been remarked upon often, women's metamorphosis into the exotic creature of the night, then shedding this transient nature like a butterfly in reverse, to emerge as pupa, as *hausfrau*. Is either of them "her real nature"? Are both, or just one, sign of her conformity—either with the *hausfrau* or the exotica? And are the exotica "individual creatures" to capture the individual mate—unique, one-off and *sui generis*? The men in this scenario are no better than stage scenery she enacts this three-act drama in front of before the footlights, with herself as audience and actor, director and producer, and beneficiary of any box office receipts. Mind you, the investment doesn't always return a profit.

304. Have some women always worn faces like that—goofy, with timid or haughty smiles hovering for a response?

305. I won't quote "carpe diem" at you, as "carpe" means "pluck" not "seize"; and the Renaissance used the saying to try to convince gals to have sex, and not to die old unmades. It seemed to work.

306. We have further relationships to give us variety in our lives, but show no variety in them; and begin to shape the new objects of our desire into identikits of the old ones, to slowly bake again on the same beach near the same sand dunes, watching the tide come in.

307. "Individuals" again? You are not the same as everyone else, so you are not the same as *anyone* else?

308. Clouds in succession—pool-shadows moving across a forest of gum trees.

309. Like children playing with the snow who've never before seen it—cold, white, dazzling—and wet.

310. Rationalism itself is not something deduced rationally, but a leap of unfaith into a world stripped bare of resonance, and articulated into separate things with space between them, and no haze confusing you as to where and what things are. It's an approach to life very common everywhere, in use for practical matters, where the aims are clear and known in advance; but was never before intended to be the only understanding of things, nor used negatively as a test for all other approaches that have ever been made; and is now reinforced by the dictum—itself without evidence—that no other approach would be possible.

Like other beliefs, it has a vision—a world in which there is no uncertainty—about things in the world or ideas in the mind. Fogs—both physical and mental—are to be isolated, so that nothing else is finally, obscured by them. And a divine clarity, and clear space, is the medium that will enable you to keep all objects distinct, even the fogs.

The logical basis for this vision would be the Aristotelian Laws of Identity—where each thing is what it is, is not what it's not, and there is no third alternative, as an Excluded Middle, between the two. These Laws have a few logical problems themselves—as the one about Relationships, or the one about Category Mistakes; but Rationalism is a belief system, and any inroads like these into it are treated like cul-de-sacs, or the work of sophist saboteurs. And the whole world is to be converted, and the feeble enemy subdued, so that the clear light of truth may pervade this universe, and be unencumbered by both the clouds of dust and the boggy marshes of superstition that these ancient marauders and their priests attempted to clog up the clarity with. It's an attractive vision of what the world could be like, but the difficulty they have convincing everyone of its viability hints, at the very least, that it's not *obviously* what the world is like; and they have never suggested any transition method for proceeding from where the world is now to this new world they are advocating, where all the problems of the old one will become obsolete.

311. "What is the meaning of a flower? What is the meaning of anything?" Things don't mean anything, and they don't mean nothing either. *Words* mean something (or some do), and things can be granted a meaning at a remove. *Then*, they don't mean nothing, because they've been granted/ bestowed/dubbed a meaning: "Arise Sir Thingaling!"

312. In argument it is important who has the right of interruption and who the right of conclusion. In love affairs it is normally the woman. In other matters some sort of authority—or "common opinion". Never is there an independent adjudicator.

313. Some arguments are as one-sided as a regimental sergeant major's "discussion" with one of his troopers. Mind you, the trooper has the right to request permission to speak. And the right to be unquestionably refused.

314. An old friend I'd lost touch with died recently—death notice in the paper. Have been feeling the prevalence of death—not my own death particularly, but death as such. Also, regret I hadn't reopened contact—though I know such things are only temporary respites for a relationship that would be in most ways obsolete. For all that, I'm feeling that *all* things are obsolete—not just myself, but everything I've been in contact with. Not yet what I *will* be in contact with—though I've no confidence there'll be any durability with things or people in the times to come either.

315. "Where does the sky end?" The vertical of the sky ends at the horizontal. Like us.

(Question from Cid Corman)

315 *int.* Some sympathy with the animism thing—that everything, say ROCK, was alive. (Corman) Trouble with a monism (EVERY thing) though, is that the contrary concept will have to ebb its way back in. In this particular case, if everything is alive, then nothing is dead—and we won't have the notion of death—or of life, that we set up against it. Or such a notion as living/ dying (Corman). And if it's only different *degrees* of living that're involved, we'll call the lower levels "death", and the upper levels "living", and we have the categories, *mutatis mutandis*, exactly as they were.

316. Mid-afternoon withdrawing towards evening. Porcelain blue faintly tinted by indigo near the horizon—except for the evening star which is white, untinted by anything.

317. You endure a lot of deaths in life through other people, before your own unrehearsed last act, and some of these deaths would be nearly as important as your own. Certainly the accumulation of them is. I've lost whole worlds, whole generations of people, and half my particular circle of friends and enemies. Those left from there are almost as devoid as I am, remnants of themselves, and have been squeegeed with me to one side of this emerging world, like garbage dropped all over the place from the night before, by another generation of revellers.

318. There's a lot of death around. But it's when one's contemporaries start disappearing (and there's a touch of black magic about it), that death makes its presence felt, as too close for comfort.

319. The bird flies directly at our window colliding with glass instead of air, to bump-recoil onto earth, to lie stunned.

320. The magpies reminding the next door neighbour it's afternoon tea time, with cuwardlings, queries at his front porch. They watch the scatter-tossings, then peck, pick their steps to the breadcrumbs over the front lawn.

321. A friend of mine, Roger Sworder, travelling by bus in Iraq several decades ago, was asked by an Arab why the Christians were polytheists (three Gods), when Allah is One. To demonstrate this Unity, the Arab made a sweeping gesture across the desert in conclusive proof.

(Checking up, it was in Turkey, though the man *was* an Arab, and the ground, though cleared and barren, was not strictly a desert—though desert enough.)

322. Myself, ironically, to Harold Stewart: "I see that they've landed on the moon". Harold in response: "Oh, that's not the *real* moon".

323. The main trouble with the concept of "God" is the presence of the three Hypostases or Personae. While "God" is thought of heretically as

only One Person. And: the character of this Person—irascible yet loving, vengeful yet forgiving, bellicose yet peaceful—is unpredictable to say the least. And not unpredictable the way a human character might be, for you can usually gauge a person's moods, both from his customary behaviour, and from the visual and auditory signs he gives out at the time, whereas "God's" moods are as unpredictable as the thunderbolt and more invisible than a gathering storm.

324. The bird's wings flurrying between sound and silence.

325. You have to be even more nit-picking about redundancies in short poems—every word must be interrogated to determine if it really has the right to its existence.

326. Some women are so attractive to men because they act like one of the boys—a better-looking version of the male, tarting a cheeky boyish image, but with attractive female accoutrements—often semi-visible.

327. Not difficult evading tags, but often difficult to evade the alternative tag that goes with it, and against it. Are you a Realist or Idealist, Christian or an Atheist, for America or against it? You make your choice, and you're tossed into the ring with this bull without a matador's cape, not sure if you're meant to be the matador or the bull—but with rowdy spectators barracking for both of you, especially the bull.

328. Then he flashes the word "God" at you like a conjuring trick or a STOP sign. And you're meant to take a detour round this line of thinking, for the road is both under construction and closed.

329. The rainbow outside itself in concentric arches—reflecting itself repetitively in fading colours.

330. The moon at last quarter sliding out of black cloud, giving body to darkness.

331. A modern tourist, journeying through the past and its remains—taking the well-known cynic route.

332. The sun leaking through at corners of the blinds.

333. I have the same birthday as Celan—*and* twelve years later. Spooky that. Great poet, but I couldn't imagine writing that stuff—"songs to be sung on the other side / of mankind".

334. A lot of academic women—in the humanities and social sciences particularly—are not so much feminists, but have *careers* in feminism.

335. The nineteenth-century literary language, with an upper class tone to lord-and-lady it over all of us.

336. At times I've felt the faint lure of the violent suicide, but I've finally little or no instinct for rabid self-destruction. Rotting's more my style.

337. The mind criss-crossing night like a border.

338. The years as they go, slip by lightly, like leaves gusted past our doors. But when they are totted up they add weight to each other, one by one in the calculation, to gain all the drag effects of decades and centuries, like piles of leaves swept off the path to be mulched.

339. Small children are both small people and cute little animals, so they can get away with ruderies that would be permitted to neither animals nor people. And their parents can have it both ways, or either way on the switch, not having to teach them to be people nor train them to be animals—as they become cute little monsters, and, like dogs, more vicious when their parents/owners accompany them.

340. I don't agree that we're "evolving"; nevertheless, you and I have to make whatever moves we make NOW—whatever *that* means—not BEFORE—however closer that was to the truth. But it wasn't closer to the truth *for us*, because in many deep as well as shallow ways, we're not there. Besides while it was closer to the truth, it was working away from it, which we in some sense have ceased to do. And finally, that truth was a relative truth anyhow, and *this* had to be recognised sometime. Whether we very limited humans are up to recognising such a starkly negative truth as this relativity (at all levels) is very dubious indeed; but that is our task if we are true intellectuals. And if we're not, we should be out of here doing something else—cabinet making or farming, for example, but not commercial law or advertising.

341. *The Triumph of the Will.* Pretty scary movie, that. Ushers in the other factor that has us "acknowledging" an "object of worship" with the rest of the congregation—terror. There must be over a million people present as the three führers lay wreaths—all completely still and silent. And there's the Orwellian touch (about the goose-step): Hitler *in himself* isn't an imposing figure—and the impulse is to laugh. But one stifles the laughter because of the threat. And the obeisance to violence that occurs because of that! And Hitler himself, ridiculous figure, becomes invested with the stifled laughter in the throat, as well as all the horrors the Nazis so openly perpetrated. The oblique, but unambiguous reference he makes to the Night of the Long Knives, with a dismissive gesture of the hand for Röhm and his massacred subordinates, is chilling.

342. The loose seed being tossed from a pan by hand to the chooks bobbing about onto it.

343. What happens after After is in the lap of the Gods.

344. As for the Imperial Power's "So help us God"—God helps those who help themselves (like Bush and Halliburton to Iraqi oil).

345. With medicine, a lot of the terms are just Latin or Greek equivalents of the English words they've ousted: "patella" just means "kneecap" and more importantly, "uterus" just means "womb" (in Latin). There's no new scientific discovery comes with this jargon, and the words shouldn't have been replaced. They were, just so educated (Latin) people ("doctors" to use another Latin word) could get purchase on it from Latin, the once universal language of education, and keep the knowledge in house. Not that most "doctors" know it now, so that for them it is as dead a language as it is for us.

I know, I was talking to a medico about stress fractures of the foot, and he used the term "navicular bone". I suggested it might come from "navis" a ship—and it was a (capsized) boat shape. So there wasn't even *that* much resonance for him.* But even if we know these terms, we learn them as without resonance. We learn them as "precise", "distinctive". O.K. with "kneecap" turning into "patella" perhaps. But what about "uterus" usurping "womb"? All sorts of human experience trashed with the term, in favour of one from a dead language that no longer has *its* resonance with it.

If I were to "purify the language of the tribe", that sort of reconnection with experience—if it could be done—would be the way I'd do it. Meanwhile, I'd like to rescue any older words I could (esp. in important areas)—older English words, that is, if only for the nostalgia.

*[*By the way this was not my own regular doctor, who's quite savvy.]*

346. There's probably a gender difference with fear and hope. Fear, particularly, excites men and depresses women. While women have gentle hopes and men wild ones. Love/sex, however, can make a difference to both these sets of reactions.

347. The creation and recognition of the Beloved is the most imaginative act in people's lives, weaving beautiful designs out of shreds of fantasy, At a deeper level, something bigger than the human is quite calculated about the biological alliances it is agitating for. But at the conscious level there is a need not to know what tribulations the prospective alliance is likely to endure, as people would be as little ready to enter into them as people would be to re-enter into them after an acrimonious divorce had sundered such an alliance.

348. The moon luminous through light cloud, then slipping clear.

349. Distinct people in a crowd? A mob of individuals.

350. The Treatise of the Golden Lion: (see Suzuki) 1. It is not true that it is. 2. It is not true that it is not. 3. It is not true both that it is and that it is not. 4. It is not true neither that it is nor that it is not.

351. Through the fern woods, the hollows' visual reverberations in green.

352. "How she managed *not* to be aware of his early proclivities." People practise such not-being-aware assiduously and secretly. You abase yourself to trust whatever this person says, or whatever this person doesn't say.

353. When she fell out with people mum could discuss their failings with pinpoint accuracy, while when they were back in favour, the sharp details would subside and disappear in a warm fuzzy vacuity. So, her knowledge of people was directly dependent upon the disaffection she felt for them

at the time, while inversely proportional to the affection she felt for them then. Or, putting it more simply, if she knew you she didn't like you, and if she liked you she didn't know you.

354. I mislaid the friendship for several years, and found it lying around while I was looking for something else.

355. Extract from Walter Benjamin, talking of Paul Klee's *Angelus Novus*, which Benjamin calls The Angel of History:

> "His face is turned towards the past. Where we see a chain of events before us, *he* sees a single catastrophe which keeps piling wreckage upon ruin till they reach his feet. If only he could stay to wake the dead and piece together the fragments of what has been broken! But a storm blows from the direction of Paradise, catching his wings with such force that the Angel can no longer close them. This storm drives him irresistibly into the future, to which his back is turned, while the pile of debris at his feet grows into the sky. This storm is what we call Progress."

356. You can make new friends, if you have the talent, till quite late in life, but it's past the time for making long-term friends.

357. A manic-depressive you say? Better than a depressive-depressive. Though this particular pendulum swings with a jerk.

358. The wind drops down through the elements as down the scales of the pan pipes.

359. Maybe the times are adjustable now. And we can solve our problems as easily as people re-set their wrist watches.

360. "If we could live 150 years, it would be grotesque and silly." (Corman) And, with the repetition, boring beyond advanced accidia. The robots would be more sprightly of mind.

361. Shadows of the rustling leaves moving about on a shadow tree.

362. Do the events you remember seem insubstantial—as if they might never have occurred? That it would have made no difference *if* they never had occurred?

363. I like the sound of a stamp—and on an ink pad too.

364. "To face whatever is." I have some sympathy for this objective. But it is by no means clear what is; and if it seems to be clear, that is not because it has been discovered, but because it has been presupposed.

365. Canvas blind flapping under a slackening wind.

366. When a friend dies it often breaks a long-standing argument you're having with him, sometimes about matters of importance. The points you want to score have no target any more, while his points hang in the air and have suddenly become unanswerable—as it's impolite, as well as impossible, to argue with the dead.

367. I nudge the silence, but realize it's left no space for me.

368. People ask whether their life has a meaning, or not. And any answer to themselves like "To get my country out of this mess" would count as one. While it is also true that the word "life" has a meaning, and we can look it up in the dictionary. But LIFE ITSELF, as opposed to the word or to a particular person's objectives in it, has no meaning. But doesn't lack one either. The application of "meaningful" or "meaningless" to it is as invalid as the application of "odorous" or "odourless" to the angle at the apex of an isosceles triangle (would you sniff it to see?), or "consonant" or "dissonant" to the main knuckle on one's own big toe. In all three cases it would be a category mistake. And you can't look up LIFE ITSELF—as opposed to the word—in a dictionary.

The whole problem arises because, following Aristotelian logic, we think that something either *is* something else, or is *not* something else, with no third alternative, an Excluded Middle, in between. But that it *can't* be something else, in this type of case, *is* that Excluded Middle.

369. Wet night, slugs about. Or snails carrying portable houses, spirals to slip into, on the sides.

370. Last week I drew up a will, and remembered hearing the superstition that such an undertaking (so to speak) is likely to bring on the event it's anticipating. Some truth in that it evokes this fear. But any documented or statistical sign of one's advancing age has a conclusive effect—even the very tappings on the shoulder of the successive birthdays themselves—or of the birthdays of our children—obviously no more significant, each of them, than the days before them and the days after them. We want to escape the definition that such events bring. In fact, we want to escape *all* definition; and death distinctly defines us—as it concludes us.

371. Hope you're getting some sleep in. None of us wants The Big Sleep, (well, not quite none); but the little death can be very refreshing, as we surface from re-immersion in it.

372. At the beach, patchy winds, willy-willies spiralling over the sand.

373. A couple of fluffs from the horn of the interstate transport. Puts lights on to open up road. Shifts gears with the staggers, to mount up the gradient past the quarry.

374. The young buck finds the single mum *very* attractive—used to sex, and enjoying it. A little later he discovers he's into a three-way relationship—the true ménage à trois—and the kids are far from having to love him—or even like him; but have got very good reason to dislike him. While there's no question which of the mother's relationships has the priority—nor ought to have.

375. You strive for the main post, not because you hanker for the main post; but because otherwise your enemy might snatch it for himself, shaft you, and leave you with no post at all.

376. After rain, the stirring up of a protracted shower of birdsong.

377. "I've made plenty of mistakes in my life, but regret none of them." (Cid) I have some regrets myself, but so often my comprehendings of situations have lagged behind the onsets of them—and there's not much you can do about that. And other mistakes come from the person I am. And at depths you can't do much about that either.

378. One puts a lot of effort into a relationship, to adapt to the person and to the relationship. They're not conveniently replaceable. Starting a new relationship—except after a considerable time—seems like infidelity—to the partner, to the relationship, and to anything substantial in you that has been involved in it; and there's something of a multiple loss. Easily moving on then, for me, seems to give conclusive evidence of my own depth shallowness.

379. I wouldn't want to live forever, because nobody else would have stayed around living forever with me.

380. And if they did we'd overcrowd the place.

381. Trees branching winds through. Spring coming up with the winds, as if out of memory. (Eliot?)

382. Whoever first exits from a relationship sets the timing of the break, and, often retrospectively, the reasons for it. For the other partner, there will be an inability to synchronize, and the relationship will be in limbo.

383. Live life to the full? I'd rather live life to the empty, and to several stages beyond overripe.

383 *int.* The Australian desert—like Australia generally—is immeasurably old. Way before—it seems—dinosaurs or the ice age—beyond imagination. We've never acclimatised. Only the kooris perhaps.

384. There's a low-level despair which enables people to continue on, with no particular reason for living, but without the impetus to terminate it.

385. Keep your eye on slabs of the pavement, with edges not flush, might catch your foot to trip you up with a kinaesthetic jolt.

386. In the middle of a drought decade, standing under a cantilever roof while steady rain falls, sniffing moisture in the air as something remembered from decades earlier, your body, blood and lungs in recognition and exultation.

CHAPTER 4

387. Death lasts longer than life. Rumours of continued life have been intermittently reported, but consistently denied—by the silence they have been met with.

388. There are a lot of paths to walk along through the temple gardens of Japan—as a pilgrim at a remove. Up the slopes at the back of Kiyo-mizudera, for one, through the articulated quiet of nature—with bird movement, whistles, rustles—set distinctly against the backdrop of a roar from modern traffic, muted beyond the hill, and subdued from the rear by the height we are at, as we mount up the slope among bird calls.

389. Astonishing how you can take your friends for granted—and are comfortable in that (and *ought* to be, perhaps). Always had some sense of the fragility of it though, and that's mainly what I perceive about me now.

390. Despite my name, I don't want youth again, with or without the Gretchen. I've been there, undone by that (though such is as it should be). As for universal knowledge?—in most senses of the phrase, no. I have most of the knowledge I can cope with now, and I'm sure it will be re-topped up to what I won't be able to cope with, yet yet again. And I certainly don't want to know everything.

391. Hope is not as strong as fear but it endures longer. Fears need to be re-stoked else they become as obsolete as threats of anarchists bombing archdukes, or of state terrorism by the guillotine. Whereas hopes will keep on rekindling themselves because they are in our genes, and ever are our nature.

392. A girl's pause, alighting from a tram, before double-jolting onto the next step, not quite judging her footing.

393. The feeling that death is inevitable and that our situation is there-fore hopeless. It comes as something like a mood. But the "hopeless" vision eventuates also because of a certain sort of logic, of rationality, of "inevitability". And when you become aware of that, you realize there are very good grounds for distrusting it. You're taking the easy, the rational way out.

394. Train with ice and sleet on the windows, adhering there for a hundred miles. Snow remaining everywhere outside, in heavy drifts and patches.

395. Not only can we adjust appropriately to our conditions, we can maladjust appropriately to them too. The conditions can be very convenient for the preferred maladjustment. So, anger-management is a required skill in civilian life, but indulging this vice will attract awards for bravery on the battlefield. And, to take another vice, many circumstances will give people an extended opportunity for being bone-lazy.

Or, trying to make yourself comfortable to sleep in the only position available might leave you in the morning with a crick in the neck. Or, stupidly, you find yourself having sex with the non-preferred sister, who happens to be more compliant, and invariably loves winning contests with her only sibling.

396. It can be a tricky business taking a compliment. It's a skill you have to learn. Insults you get much more practice at; so you can grow a very horny integument against them. It's like bathing in the dragon's blood, and you're invulnerable.

397. Hedgefuls of birds and twitter.

398. A nostalgia, much more poignant, for those events that never did occur.

399. Very often us oldies are treated as quasi-dead—though not with the fear one might have expected from such apparitions. I suppose more like wisps of ghost rather than Frankenstein monsters or Golems or unwrapped bodies fresh from the opened coffins.

400. Henry Ford: "History is bunk." And now the man himself is history.

401. The traditional view sees no evolution, but only devolution from the Centre. The devolution goes first to the North (in our cycle), the phase of Urizen in Blake's *Zoas* (Urizen = your-reason), then to the other three compass corners—with the Centre, in some sense, moving to each compass point with each move. So that one goes from the integration of all, at the original centre, to concentration on each of the four main

sectors of the cycle in turn—facets corresponding to the four seasons as well as the faculties of man (the reason, the intuition, the passion, and the body's sense of itself).

The whole thing is more confused at the end of the cycle—where we are now, I believe—(during the intercalary time)—when there is no longer concentration on one of the Quarters, or, microcosmically, Faculties (their times having been phased out) but negatively on the Centre itself, in which there are no longer faculties, or positives, modifying the Absolute. Originally there was also no particular quality etc., but the whole-of-them-plus, in integration—but that's positively, when they were still about to be manifested—while lastly it's about to be "revealed" negatively that finally all positives are as nothing.

402. Do we forget the dead, because it's the polite thing to do?

403. NOTHINGS can also be significant. A little oppressive sometimes, when they close down around you, but liberating at others when they open out in front of you. I like mobile nothings—like gusty days. And still ones can be good too—with trees around them, and a cockatoo or two to punctuate the silence.

404. Authority is being carefully sequestered from all but the administrators—from parents, from teachers, not quite yet the police—so that the overlords can make their judgments from afar, and not be touched by the local consequences, nor have to endure coming in contact with distasteful manifestations of poverty and death. And those at the local workplaces need to harden their hearts so that they can match the "objectivity" of these distant overlords.

405. I am no longer tempted to put the Absolute and love so close together; and now see love as a series of events within the seasonal cycle, like all of life's affairs.

406. Organising the Los Angeles Olympic Games: "Well gentlemen, we don't want to over-commercialise the Games, but we don't want to *under*-commercialise them either". So—they commercialised them.

407. Invisible web with daddy long legs spider upon it, away from the wall, on which extended shadow daddy long legs spider scuttles, elongated on the light and synchronising with the original.

408. Our Bugle-call-for-the-military-dead day. Somehow, the Last Post for the young men that have died becomes as well an affirmation of the justice of the wars that killed them—lest we forget that. So that we can be certain they did not die "in vain". And the very un-dead army platoons are there in all their pomp, to carry us along through slow-then-quick marching, to the sound of the brass band and the thump of the bass drum, and the insistent rhythms of the marching feet. (La Grande Illusion)

409. The "no fly zone". Really? They've even exterminated the flies?

410. And Wall Street has its biblical phrase too: "A Den of Thieves". Haven't heard that one yet from the "Christian Fundamentalists", who keep fossicking about in the Old Testament for very obscure phrases to get literal with.

411. In the Catholicism of my youth you were meant to be piously dumbfounded about matters of faith and morals—and mores—and listen reverently to whatever canon laws the local parish priest was discharging on such matters. Unless you were a canonised saint. But then, inconveniently, you didn't become canonised (and only by the institution of which this priest was the local representative) until you were dead. A little hubris, most would have thought, to pre-empt the issue, so you went along with Holy Church, saint or not. There were also the Pope and the cardinals, not exactly canonised, but authoritated and legitimated. No hubris there—they just happened to be always right—while the saints were right in arrears, where it no longer counts.

412.

413. The message in most right-wing violence films—where the mass carnage and mayhem is justified as revenge for something horrible that's happened to the girl friend, wife or children earlier in the film. Then the joyous abandon and orgasm of the brutalisms in response.

414. A false sense of security is better than no sense of security at all.

415. Tree-shadows tidalled over by scudding cloud-shadows.

416. OK. There was no Golden Age—from which we've all degenerated. And so this is no Dark Age. Nor a Golden One, from which we will degenerate. Golden Age or Dark Age enough? Or the Nondescript Age?

417. You learn something, in undergoing poverty? Trouble is, you never see it distinctly, because you're up to your neck and mouth in it, treading water, or beginning to sink beneath it.

418. Other day, snow field on the park surrounded by spruces—like a still pond of snow. Edging into the trees, isolating them from each other.

419. The Machiavellian prince is not bound by morality; because he is effectively a state. And because other states are not bound by morality—only people within moral jurisdictions—this state would be at a disadvantage if it alone were to be bound by one.

The businessman sees himself as in the same predicament as the prince or state. If he acts morally he puts himself at a disadvantage in a world of business where morality has no place. That's why they speak of it as a "jungle" that is allegedly out there. Mind you, when this becomes the business ideology, it is also more true in practice—though no more true in principle—and they've deliberately built a paltry excuse into this ideology, to exculpate themselves in advance from any immorality they might indulge in out there.

420. The tobacconist shop—odours of tobacco. Next door, barber, smell of cut hair.

421. "I doubt if he (Michael Schmidt) knows that you exist." I have my own doubts about that.

422. One of the joys with kids is to see them vibrantly snapping up our platitudes of understanding as their own discoveries, their minds opening out to a world of new truths—ones we can be very comfortable with. It's called "Educating the Young". Later, in adolescence, they see the deficiencies in such platitudes, and make us quite uncomfortable with their barbs. For they have moved with the times, and can now understand such platitudes—though not yet their own—to be as time-affected as they always were.

423. When old, people treat you as if you had a contagious disease—which you have, in a way. Though I bet most of them would prefer the disease to the cure.

424. I begin to feel I have given too little weight to the living realities, and the people, that have come in and out of my life. I've not seen anybody able to gravitate the passing of time however, and of worlds and of people; yet for the first time now consider their distress and unbalance might be more appropriate than my own facile poise (or deep poise, if I were able to maintain it in a balance), however unfacile its genesis and its justifications might have been.

425. A set of the jaw, as if she'd just stopped chewing gum, which sits in the corner of her mouth while she waits for someone stupid enough to hazard a remark she can blitz her counter-attack on.

425 *int*. Where did my dead friends go? Into the stars, and to the unfathomable spaces between.

426. Our loves and close friendships will mimic family relationships—father/daughter, brother/sister, mother/son—and give them a tremolo they mightn't otherwise have had. But these relationships do not need to be symmetrical. So, one person might have the other as father figure, while the other might see her as younger sister—for such asymmetry as quite compatible with the relationship's harmonious balance.

427. "Serial Marriage" (B.F.) has become so conventional it's corny—and very flaky. Cornflakes.

428. Shop windows' reflected images, that slip along the outside as if along the inside, behind aquarium glass.

429. Is the Western-cum-universal mode of thought two-dimensional rather than three-dimensional—not in depths but at shallows? Is it a thinking with pencil sketchings and rulings on a drawing board?

430. But language has "open texture", for the meanings are re-adjustable—otherwise it would have no history—and it does. It's like the open-endedness of actions, that don't always come up with the

same consequences, or move about in exactly the same way. The only alternative is leading our lives so as to repeat other lives, and others' speech, allowing nothing but the repetition. That of course—though hardly uncommon—is demented. (Waissman)

431. By the gate a bushfull of birds—chirruping in undulations.

432. John Phillips has asked for "a few well-placed Australian curses". They don't go well on paper. You have to be leaning against the bar, a beer in one hand, letting them slip through near-closed lips and clenched teeth (to keep the flies out)—and "laconic" is hardly the word. For the older Australians were best at understatement—irony, chyacking were their vein. And you left your hat on in the bar—to hide the bald spot—and probably in bed, too (an old one, with splits in the corners of the dinge).

433. The dogs depositing turds not on wet grass but on dry, to keep their bums unwetted.

434. Some crap thinking here. Try the following: "This model of radical openness creates poems that are empty at the centre; instead of seeing poetry as a vessel for the poet's self-expression, it privileges the removal of self from the concerns of the poem".

So? You get rid of the self, just like that? Buddhists work a lifetime on ANATTA ("non-self", close enough), but working *through* a "self" of some sort (and there *is* an empirical reality here, however delusional finally) to get there. And the "there" is no stopping place, but a TAO, a VIA. These fellahs think they can have it easy, with a simple denial (note the "instead of"—as if there were only two possibilities here—one of them being the late Romantic "guy gotten into the landscape").

And what happens when you have done all this excision—of the Romantic self and its language? Well, they'll metamorphose, as such things always do—especially when you try to dodge them or excise them—it's like trying to dodge around or excise yourself.

Well known, all this—and not just in Buddhism. Try the following, from La Rochefoucauld about "l'amour-propre" ("self-love" or "self interest").

"Nothing is so vehement as its desires, nothing so concealed as its aims, nothing so devious as its methods; its sinuosities beggar the imagination, its transformations surpass metamorphoses, its complications go beyond that of chemistry. …it performs a thousand imperceptible twists and turns…"

So with self-love, so with the self, so with "self-expression". If you duck the issue like this—or swerve around it, pretending to yourself you're pushing on straight ahead, you'll drive right through it all right, but yet again emerge on the same side. (Penguin trans., L. Tancock 1959.)

435. Gull finds pocket of air to glide through, and on, wheeling to a curve; wing tip dangles. Wheels again, wrenches up to start of a widening spiral.

436. Victorian houses with a century-old whiff about them. As if the nineteenth-century inhabitants had remained alive, still occupying them: the men dressed in nineteenth-century cloth, starched linen, stiff pointed collars digging into their necks; the women with long heavy brocaded dresses sweeping footpaths and floors.

437. The moon back-scudding through clouds. Everything lightens, then darkens.

438. That Achilles Fang story *is* funny. You ain't worldly-wise enough for a Jesuit. Your *a*-theology, on the other hand, would be *no* problem. And no Holy Poverty for that mob—even in principle. How on earth did St Francis survive in the Church? (I know the Jesuits weren't around then, but their sort of thinking was always around.)

439. "Be optimistic, look to the future."
    "I look into the future and I see darkness. Better stay where we are."
    "But you can't."
    "O.K. Then we'll take account of the future when it comes."

440. I've taken my own human losses much too heavily in the last few years: it's a danger with people like us. Mind you, how heavily one *ought* to take them is a question. *Pretty* heavily, I would think—but have no real answer. "Let the dead bury their dead" is too frightening now for me to contemplate. Even though it itself is long-standing folk wisdom, it shows both how practical and how ruthless people have always been, at the death.

441. "…where does space end?…" Don't know what you (or Kant) mean by "where".

441 *int.* "…where does space end?…" Where does space begin?

442. Minah lands and pauses—bird-body bends flexible twig-body.

443. You've got your fixed position. You can argue from it, but you've never argued to it. So you give *me* no reason to argue to it, while I'm certainly not going to argue from it.

444. One of the commonplace assumptions is that solid ordinary people don't philosophize, but only intellectual wankers spouting airy-fairy nonsense. On the back of this assumption, the commonplace philosophical positions are seen as "obvious", "realistic" and the rest—not as positions at all. It *should* cause queries, when such positions change; but the later arrivals into the commonplace just see (as always) the *contemporary* positions as being, "obvious", while the older positions are something we've grown out of—if they're different. Following such conventional thought patterns, most people, without knowing it, do quite a bit of philosophizing, and even (sometimes quite bad) logic. So there *is* a place for logical correctives in "real life"—which is often a lot more airy-fairy than that phrase would normally have us believe.

445. We bury people's bodies quickly for hygiene, because they rot; but why do we bury their memories so quickly, when they've already begun to dissipate and wisp away?

446. Amazing that we tend to think that *any* time people die is the appropriate time for them to die. It certainly wouldn't seem the appropriate time for *us* to die, and perhaps for those closest to us. With children and the young the logic is different: it certainly isn't the correct time for them to be dying—they have not lived long enough, and are not yet defined. But at a mature age, even in mid-life, the person does seem so defined, and death gives a punctuation point to the definition.

447. I've found that, after a very long time not answering a letter, the excuse required to explain the delay becomes the final reason for not answering it.

448. Will Christ's adjudication at the Last Judgment be to the letter of the Law? And would the Accused have the right to Council for the

Defence when he is being prosecuted by the Crown? Then, will the adversarial system be used, so that if his barrister were wily enough in his legalistic interpretations, the Accused would go "free", on presumption of innocence? Or is the trial under the Great Judge merely a show trial—the verdict already decided?

449. The uninvited cats living under the house next door scratched away at the ducted heating pipes to give themselves blow-warmth, while the people above shivered through winter.

450. To have a lot of relationships teaches how little any of the people involved meant to you, and how little substance in you was there, after being intermingled in so many relationships.

451. The stone lantern lit by a candle at night—fluttering yellow light behind white paper within stone.

452. Considering how long you've survived above ground, they bury you in it quickly.

453. Christians' beliefs were instituted as state law under Constantine, and non-belief effectively became criminalised. So the Creed became statute—to be conformed to, by the letter. Beliefs such as "Christ is the Son of God" firmed into clauses in legislation. No point in *contemplating* them, you just adhered to them; and your understanding was handcuffed and fettered right there to prevent it from wandering off across any of the borders, or even just straying within them, to confuse either the security forces or the police. (Schuon)

453 *int*. But I want to know whether or not she still likes me, and whether it was *really* a negative sign when I saw her lip curl.

454. We assess an event by what is accomplished, not by what's done to accomplish it. So will, most usually, underestimate the time spent in completing the activities, when men's bodies have to physically negotiate the spaces, the materials, the work implements and the terrain to finish whatever has to be done, not like us, tracing it out to analyse it, in pencil sketchings and ruled lines across an office drawing board.

455. From the bird's throat a rapidly corrugated note.

456. Like the float in a lavatory cistern—looking solid as that's emptying when the toilet's flushed; but lightweight when the cistern refills and the ball's refloated.

457. The gambits of the smooth-talking men with women are so obvious that there is no question of any savvy woman being deceived by them. The women *need* the attempts to be so blatant so that any exercise of their own discrimination simply cannot arise—and they can slide down this primrose path without consulting their brains one tiny bit about the matter.

458. Stroking the back of the times hoping they purr.

459. The wet leaves that have slipped into the crevices last a lot longer than any season passing over them.

460. All our thinking words (excepting "think" itself) and most of our feeling ones are metaphorical—"see", "understand", "enlighten", "track it down", "feeling" itself, "distinguish", "separate" (as in space), "conclusion", "elucidate", "it breaks my heart", "I'm stunned by it", "well-grounded". The Latinate ones don't look it, and not just because we can't construe Latin, but because people need to "look at things objectively", and don't want to think of their methods and categories of understanding as having a metaphorical base. And the Latinate words can seem so much more objective because their metaphorical base is in an unknown dead language. Though even in a living language the metaphor will go dead—as in "understand" (stand under), or in "base" itself.

461. "A.F. (Achilles Fang) claimed God never existed in China." (Corman) The whole package certainly, but I'm not sure the *whole* package existed anywhere (except in St. Thomas's noodle?). Quite a few items from the package even in China, I would have thought.

462. And Achilles Fang was a bit naive about the Jesuits, thinking they might have invited you in (intelligence wasn't enough). The ones he was thinking of were free-thinking ON TOP OF the thoroughly well-trained religious-order-commissioned-officer, cum intellectual task force, cum political and social casuist that was the ordained Jesuit. You were cannier

than A.F. in not even thinking about it. (*I* had the offer in fact, but knew more, from my upbringing, what it meant.)

463. I wonder if you can undercut Occam's Razor—showing that the category of Unnecessary Metaphysical Entities is itself an unnecessary metaphysical entity? The unkindest undercut of all? Probably not—as it's a negative not a positive—and so not an entity as such, but a useful rule of avoidance, to cut our metaphysical costs.

464. "The just man sinneth seven times daily." While the unjust man (myself) would do well to avoid sinning, seven times daily. And even then I'd need some help.

465. I did complain to friends—though not to her—that mum's longevity was restricting me from moving on into my own old age. Suddenly I'm here, and have my wish. So serve me bloody well right.

466. The full languidness of youth. It's got all the time in the world to be lolled through.

467. "Life is nothing … Meaningless. Pointless. Hopeless." If life is nothing, what is the something that it is not? What's being *denied* by "Life is Nothing", and consequently, what is being affirmed? What is the *meaning* that it is not, what is the *point* that it is not?

 As for "hopeless", people will have hope, or lack it, whatever the circumstances. "Grounds for hope" won't be needed by the hopeful, and will be interrogated then denied by the hopeless or the skeptics.

468. You've had your chance at youth and wasted it. You'd want another chance, to waste it again?

469. My late friend Harold Stewart used to say: "You don't grow old, you get pushed into it". And your children, particularly, shove you out of the way when they occupy life. (And it's better than you leaving your bloated body there, to block up space.)

470. The word "God" like a STOP sign on the road telling us it's dangerous to proceed. And we turn back trying to figure out how to get to our destination some other way. Perhaps they should have put the stop sign

outside of the destination itself, and we might have heard news of it. Or better still, erected it outside of the home we left to come here. And we would never have set off on this fiasco of a journey.

471. "Bullshit" is obviously a sexist term. Its collaterals would be "cowshit"—there's a fair bit of that spread around—"calfshit", and "heifershit"—a less mature form of cowshit.

472. Optimism and Pessimism. Any whiff of the latter is complained about by people hearing anything "negative" they believe they oughtn't to approve of. And they're scared *even to hear it*. Shows that *they* are really pessimistic in exactly the way they don't want themselves to hear about.

473. Alzheimer's is the aged's disease of choice. You've got a lot more people and things to remember than when you were young, so you need to slough quite a bit of it, to recall just the important things. But the important things don't seem as important as they once did, so why recall anything at all?

474. Bees around, dangling off one flower to another—back-muzzling in, buzzleing. Paused.

475. Drought years. The reservoir banks deep as a quarry site. Only a couple of separate puddles at the bottom.

476. Unfortunately, we judge people mainly on how they treat people like us—principally on the evidence of how they actually *do* treat us.

477. A Freudian sex dream is often like an unsophisticated ribald joke. The occasional one I had when young was in colour—when I normally dreamt in black and white—with postmen posting letters in letter boxes and buildings on fire—and myself rushing around with all the joyous abandon of a pyromaniac and a fireman hosing things down, both.

478. She did have the women's sentimentality (and quite proper) about her kin, especially the babies and future generations. Not the middle class women's sentimentality about *the psychological*—psychological sensitivities, traumas and the rest. Too practical, too no-nonsensical and, thank God, too undermiseducated for that.

This comment too is perhaps outdated. Psychological jargon is now so diffused through the culture, that undermiseducation is no longer a bulwark against it.

479. Psychological Feeling. Curious to speculate which of its physical correspondences—and prior word usages—it derives from. The "feeling" that is the palpable touch, contacting the surrounding world; or the "feeling" when the surrounding world impacts on your body; or the "feeling" of the body when it becomes ill or there is something medically wrong; or the physical exhilaration or depression when psycho-somatic events stir the pot or turn the gas off.

480. The idea of "God" is a mobile concept. It shifts from immanent to transcendent and back again, from abstract to personal and back again, from uni-personal to tri-personal and back again, confusing the issue and dodging theological bullets—and accusations of heresy backed by torture and the stake. While the confusion thus created is meant to be a "mystery of religion"—that you are meant to get very genuflective about—rather than theological chaos. In its wake, certain doctrinal necessities—like the Three Persons of the Trinity—truncated into one domineering overlord that you are meant, cringingly, to love—become devotionally inoperative.

481. The role model for boys in the single mum's family is the male vagrant and his replacement blow-in.

482. Hardly any of us in tourist lounges, but have touched down at birth, and lived away from the airport, near where something's still left of a rural countryside. While at the airport itself, the next plane hasn't landed yet, and will neither be crash-landing, nor taxiing on in to accommodate folk. While people loll about on lounges or do nothing in particular, to while away the time and wait for their flights. Nevertheless, wherever people are, things are in motion.

483. You make your own bad luck whenever your friends and enemies will have forgotten to make it for you.

484. All cures are temporary. Mind you, temporary is where we live.

485. Clouds travelling slower than the wind—on weightlessness.

486. We "reasonablists" have the feeling that the past was dark and evil except on the fringes, where the truth was being painfully born. Evil usually because of some particular viciousness—violence, patriarchy, repression (including psychological) or superstition. And that it would all hang around like a foul smell, or at best a musty odour, before it was blown away by the fresh winds of today.

487. The most important thing you learn in the academy is why it's not to be overestimated. It's something you need to learn, for all that. There are some modest virtues in scholarship, and the "popular" view of it ("wankers") is inadequate. Their own view of themselves, however, is as overinflated as the paper bag they are forever about to pop.

488. People get disgusted at the idea of the Romans' "vomitorium"— where they tickled their throats on the inside with a feather, to spew up so they could recontinue eating. Very sensible of them to have their gourmet and gluttonous pleasures with few of the after-effects. Much like our use of contraceptives, or the morning-after pill.

489. The creation of the Beloved is the one really imaginative act in most people's lives; but further on, such creations tend to have the predictability of out-of-date pop songs—that people once made love to, but are now at best tuning forks for nostalgia.

490. For all that, even though she agreed she'd missed me—when asked— there were no enquiries as to whether I had missed her.

491. Paul on whether "enlightenment" is sudden or gradual or recurrent. Jan Bender's suggestion certainly describes what normally seems to happen—where people *have* insights, and realizations of being, but then find that such realizations fade, lapse, become past their use-by date for what's happening later on, sometimes even become obstacles to progress on The Way. Any realization is, in some sense, out of time, so—unless we synchronize it with our own deaths—if we are to continue living we move on from it, or are *moved* on from it. And the goal is an interim goal anyhow.

From the psychological point of view (or "pneumatological" point of view—Coomaraswamy's coinage) this can be usefully bracing, so that you don't loll around in comfort after the "achievement"; but it can also

75

be depressing, when time takes away any advancement pretty much completely. And you are recommencing again and again on the path from exactly the same spot. And life is like that—in both its sacred and its profane worlds, and in the nebular worlds between them.

492. A close friend's death removes a lot of one's own experience with it, and corroborations of memories and mutual impressions. Your own memory bank has been robbed overnight.

493. Moth's fumble-flight across screen door, with blurring wings.

494. There's a lot of death around. A one hundred per cent strike rate. *That's* pretty impressive.

495. Apart from their reactionary politics—in practice backing any brutalising right wing authority—the main trouble with the most impressive of the trad. doc. authors, Guenon, is the stark dichotomy he makes between Purusha (Essence) and Prakriti (Substance) and the sense of the Holy War to be waged for the first and against the second (and their derivatives for words and ideas—"Nama" and "Rupa"). As well as the *lack* of sense of the Yang-yin principle and of the idea of timely correct blended approaches to the particular correct route on The Path at any one time. (Mind you, I'm not talking about compromise—you ought to *take* that correct route then, without deviating to the right or left of it at all.)

496. With people we have known, the deaths don't cancel each other out and displace each other, but keep accumulating and add up to an unforgettable stockpile. Owen's death has not displaced Frank Samperi's, even momentarily, nor Ian's. "Since he hath all my brothers tane." But I will try to hang on still—if by the toes not the neck.

497.

498. I took friendship for granted when young. I never understood how frequently ten year gaps would intervene, and how difficult we would find it then fitting the broken pot of a friendship back together again—with different pieces.

499. Death doesn't round things off. All its relationships are rent jagged-edged through the middle.

500. Peter was the only son of an Austrian archduke who had emigrated from Austria during the thirties—I'm not sure whether or not before the Anschluss—and had settled in Melbourne, completing an engineering degree and working as a civil engineer there. He was known locally, with affectionate and respectful irony, as The Prince of Perhapsburg.

501. The rope thrown from the fishing boat onto the quay, by a fisherman who leapt up and across to loop-fasten it onto a close-at-hand bollard.

502. Not only is it true that our knowledge of people is impression only, but the reality of people is impression only, whether anyone's having the impressions or not.

502 *int.* Constantine's move to incorporate the State within Christianity, and Christianity within the State was politically very astute—promoting social conformity, with this very personal religion, even in the depths of the person. Religiously, of course, it was disastrous—so that, *even in the depths of the person*, you were permitted only conformity.

503. No doubt one has to *concentrate* on the poetry, all right, else it won't get done, *at depth*. On the other hand, one knows one's got the balance wrong if one has experience so one can write poetry about it. The lesser version we are all liable to—picking over one's own life far too much and often for what's actually available there. So—I had a period a few years ago when I wrote about significant incidents I'd been carrying in my head and heart since my boyhood and youth. Almost all of them came up well, so I was tempted to go looking for other material from then to fill out an opus. I *did* try once or twice, but it was a stupid thing to do. The original ones had chosen me, over many years; now I was trying to choose them—and it wasn't the *poet* in me making the choice.

504. Light from the headlamps dipping into the bottom of the hill, then sliding back to horizontal up the other slope.

505. K563. Probably I needed not just the key, but the keyhole and a door to enter it. Reminds me of one of those De Chirico buildings— pyramidal except for a square architectural lantern at the top, while the shadows are at odd angles, with a girl skipping to a skipping rope, and a tiny steam engine with still puffs of smoke in the distance. Where the problem is: *it's in another time* (and always was).

506. How can you plumb the depths when everything, including yourself, is in motion? Like attempting to cast a line then fish, out of a speedboat at full throttle.

507. When the rabid right wing of American politics shouts "Over my dead body!", they do mean "Over *your* dead body", don't they?

508. "The American way of life is not negotiable." (George Bush Snr.) And would it be non-negotiable for the Americans too?

509. Wittgenstein examines one of the "feelings", pain, as a possible example of necessarily private information that can't be questioned, contradicted or qualified, from the "outside", and that demonstrates, as it were, a private world of the "individual". I guess more recent modes (of psychology, sociology and the like) have worn down this sense of unique people with radically different internal worlds that we're hankering for different messages from. I'm in half of two minds about it (at least). But, if the messages are *so* distinctive, what sense can other people make of them, out of the absolute privacy of these interior monologues? or, if they are commonplace, why expect any more than well-phrased platitudes, resounding back to what you "know" completely already?

510. I'm not looking for compliments. And I don't want to hear your insults. So am not interested in anything you've got to say about me—or in fact about anything.

511. A few chirrups from birds, spray-droplets across silence.

512. I heard X used to preface his poetry readings with Buddhist mantras recited (if I remember) to a gong. But those syllables were meant for a *ritual*, not for a vaudeville act. (O.K. Ginsberg doing something like that—*he* was just trying to be nice to the universe.)

513. In Western thinking, distinctions distinguish one thing from another (or one "concept"-thing from another), a first from a second—which it is not. So already you have the makings of a quasi-arithmetical logic that we inherited from the Scholastics, with Identity—"this thing *is* that thing"—and contradiction—"this thing is *not* that thing"—and arguments as to whether this identification you are making is "in fact"

a contradiction or not. Whether this is the same one thing as that, or whether it is a second thing and different, "distinguishable". Each "thing" is one thing—and not a second, and has either to be it or not to be it, with no third alternative.

514. Alzheimer's etc.? But meaning gets drained away, and not just by you—you are deprived of it by others too. However, any meaning that has been drained away—your family, social position, status, relationships, function—was never there.

515. Clumps of hail left along the path side, rain softly hammering at it.

516. I walk out into gusts as into a bonhomie of the Gods that I'm too flustered to join or not to join.

517. A lot of the modesty that young women once seemed to have had was just diffidence. Now that modesty is no longer conventional, they might be obliged to show their conformity with what once would have been immodesty. So, social diffidence might have them modest in one era, and immodest in another.

517 *int.* In modern times, we tend to see Today as the beginning of Tomorrow, whereas it's more likely to be the end of Yesterday.

518. And the "theological" vision that has timelessness in heaven and endless time in hell is playing sadistic games with people's hearts, dreaming up fantastical punishments for them to concentrate on—both the infernals and the spectators. A strange vision to have the Blessed in Heaven *rejoicing* at the agony inflicted on the Damned. "But they're inflicting it on themselves" seems a hollow excuse for the onlookers' delight in such torture. And don't give me any stuff about "justice". "Let him who is without sin among you cast the first stone." "But Jesus Christ, we're just having a peek-a-boo.
    And technically speaking, we're actually without sin now."
    There is also the question of how, in timelessness, they can witness the progression of punishments in time.

519. Laying a carpet is not easy. With some women I've known sufficiently well, I would have needed an amnesty in advance *in writing* before attempting such a task.

520. Still, life goes on. Let's hope I go on with it. Really?

521. Particularly about human relationships, you learn retrospectively from experience—often futilely. You learn what you should have done, not what you still have to do.

522. Sex between other people is perhaps the greatest of all comedies—hilarious, frequently ridiculous. While our own sex is normally the most serious of matters. It may occasionally become hilarious without penalty, but we are flirting with danger if it turns to the ridiculous. For it is certainly that. And you and your partner may never again forget it.

523. A knock on the door at two o'clock in the morning while I was still awake. Went to the door and interrogated the outside with "Who's there?" Answer: "The Police". And I searched my guilt for whatever illegality had occurred on my shift, but opened the front door, leaving the gridded fly wire door still snipped.
     They'd caught somebody bashing in the grille on my car, after receiving a telephone call from my next-door neighbour a quarter of an hour earlier. By the time I emerged to survey the damage, he'd been head-shoved inside a police car with flashing blue lights and a full beam from headlights.
     Had been crawling on and around the next door neighbours', demanding to be let in; but, it not being the hour for a social call, my neighbours, Pat and Cahline, phoned the police instead. As he attempted to gain entrance there, he'd been muttering/shouting "Who put this house here?" Apparently he lived in a parallel street two blocks further along the connecting road, and initially thought he'd been locked out—but realized they'd changed the house not the locks. He'd been drinking from ten o'clock the afternoon before. I've been drunk a few times in my life, but never so pissed to the eyeballs as to think they'd swap my house around in the middle of the night.

524. What heat! At least if I melted into a puddle on the pavement, I'd dry up quickly.

525. Some married couples have a devious tag-team approach to others, so that, for example, unprovoked nasty comments about you can often be more appropriately attributed to the spouse *not* making them than to the spouse who is.

526. I'm getting to a stage in life where there's been a general massacre among my relatives and friends. It's what awaits the "long life" that we are continually wishing people. Nevertheless we want it; and probably would still want it if we could see all that it entailed, and our reactions to that. Plenty of people to tell us what is to occur, but they know it's boring (usually) and don't say. Besides we wouldn't listen to them, but need/want to experience it for ourselves—so we believe. And we think we know already. Oh, Really?!

527. "The market always gets it right in the long run". So, in the short run, the market gets it wrong? Or is it that whenever it gets it right *is* the long run? And if it hasn't got it right yet, how long could the long run be?

528. This line of reasoning about the markets is far too obvious to have remained unnoticed. So why *has* it remained unnoticed? Is it because people avert their eyes from it, as they would from criticism of religious beliefs? Is the dictum about the markets an utterance to give us all economic hope, and to check any emerging fear—after having first created it?

529. Any person can be competitive. All people can be competitive. And what is it to be competitive?—to win against people who are losing. So, if no people are losing, no people are winning either, and *nobody* is competitive.

530. The powers-that-be are certainly aware of this particular psycho-sociologic, and have encouraged rebellious styles in fashion, in music, clothes and attitudes, to divert any latent rebellion into frivolous pursuits. In fact, they have corralled both the rebellion and the reaction to it into a self-contained ricochetting dialectic, which can't escape out into the free world of ideas, where that reality might have disrupted the dialect's internal patterning and re-patterning.

531. What we have been trying to trace is not a logic, but a para-logic: the set of entailments, inferences, and indeed opinions that seem unarguably correct to a particular group, class or era, its "para-reasoning". Any external standard of rationality, applied to these matters, must be from someone who is lost in theory, and has no longer any contact with the real world—is what such a group will automatically assume.

532. The first drops of rain—small dark pockmarks upon the earth.

533. Most "learning from experience" is retrospective—or if you are melancholy, introspective. We'd usually prefer it to be prospective.

534. Easing the beads of her rosary between middle finger and thumb, steadied by a forefinger, as she mumbles her responses to the litany.

534 *int*. Waiting for a train back to Bendigo on a country platform by myself. Vacant land owned by the railway across the fence on the opposite platform—with gum trees and a temporary pond from recent rain. No cars going past. And I remember the silence of the bush.

535. Kierkegaard "…the empirical object is unfinished and the existing cognitive spirit … thus the truth becomes an approximation…". Definite point in logic here, but I'm not sure he's placed it at exactly the right spot. Actually, Hume points out that, effectively, even the approximation can't be made "absolutely", or "exactly" (*viz*,. finally, at all), that we can't posit what a thing or event "probably" is, because we are relying on data always from the past, where what-it-is is "unfinished" (as K says). Or, putting it another way, we have expectations about an object's continuance, written in to our ideas of what it is; and yet there's no reason why the future will be like the past, and the objects in it—not even mainly like it, or "probably" like it, or "approximately" like it. *We* might want to call it by the same name, looking forward to it from here; but even if in the future they call it by the same name, the name itself might not mean the same, as they might well have accommodated the same language to the new denotations and connotations it would have developed by then.

536. To have to continually reinflate hope must be a drain on one's energy, whereas pessimism can afford to be smug.

537. Rain knocking the cherry blossoms off the trees, so we lower our eyes to walk through cherry blossom sludge.

538. Spiritual knowledge is taken to be a learning of what is *not* the case. That's not an accumulation of knowledge in the ordinary sense, but is there something cumulative about it? And this, in spite of the fact that there will be sometimes a turning back on many of your own

accumulated negative realizations? Would a simple arithmetic tot up an accumulation of numerous unknowings, cancel out some, then get the finally revised additions or subtractions right.

539. Nothing endures—not even emptiness. For a void, as such, wouldn't have substance either, nor duration. It would be internally mobile, shifting on into something, back to nothing, then on on again.

540. There are several earlier "maturities" in life. We pass through them like railway stations in a train, with refreshment rooms at each station; yet, while there *is* an end of the line, there's no further station there.

541. The neons winking, unscrolling—at the entertainment centre across the park.

542. As for poets, do we "marry the brewer's daughter"? (Novalis), and be appointed to the Board of the Brewery? Or even become the brewer himself?—the vatic solution.

543. Winter boughs, branches' top side glazed in ice. Icicles below. Water drops hanging from the icicles—one, several. Frost-snow in grass on the railway embankment. Snow down below with sheen across, more silk than satin, in smooth but humped sheets.

544. I've been an—unobservant—spectator for most of my life—just making up the numbers.

545. So long since you've heard from me I might as well be dead. And perhaps I am that—some tales have the dead wandering around not realizing they *are* dead, till the accumulated evidence finally insubstantiates it for them.

546. Not only is everything transient, but the transiency is at such *depths*. If one needed to have the ephemeral, you'd at least expect it to be superficial, and not excavate so deep.

CHAPTER 5

547. Are the alternatives to be over-satisfied with what we are, or deeply dissatisfied? The choice hyperconfidence, or despair?

548. There is also a laughter with the presumption how right we are, and how correct was the exclusion of this person or object by our laughter. There is no particular humour in this laughter, only self-congratulatory contempt.

549. When a woman says "I don't love you any more", she is often making the first and final announcement of her decision, ratified on the spot, not just to the man she is abandoning, but to herself. Though often too, she has made the decision beforehand, and has already moved on to another partner, either in speculation or in act. And other times, she's just tired of the effort in love.

550. She landed the counter-punch before the punch. Goodness knows if there otherwise would have *been* a punch, to validate this counter-punch.

551. We need consolation for the real horrors and losses that life brings; consolation is too precious a gift to be offered to jittery apprehensiveness about trivial matters. Mind you, sometimes the trivial matters are a substitute for more profound ones, which are far too overwhelming to be faced up to.

552. Orwell and La Roche on the unexpected virtues of hypocrisy. The paying of even lip service to a principle is better than having none—let alone having none on principle. Though the last can sit very comfortably with hypocrisy's own mode of manipulation.

553. A cloud making billow along wind—puff-white with silver edgings.

554. I notice that when you've created space for yourself, other people will find room to move into it.

555. Faithfulness needs continuity—which means contact, not sporadic telephone calls from distant continents: and I feel hanging in the air—like a phone off the hook.

556.

557. The parents saying "I love you" is more complex, of course. (And, of course, completely anachronistic for earlier times.) Some sense of loss involved there, I think. After all, parental love translates as duty, not as expressions of affection, and this was once obvious; and at some level perhaps, still is.

558. A ball tossed up, then comes back to hand—the drop of the ball and the drop of the hand synchronising on the catch.

559. "Bless her soul" doesn't mean I think there are souls, for I don't. When Wittgenstein was asked whether he believed in God, he replied: "Well, I can say 'God bless you', and *really* mean it.

560. Metaphor defined in distinction from simile as a comparison that doesn't use "like" or "as", the way the simile does. It seems too open-weave a net to trawl for the very exotic fish that poets fill their oceans with.

561. Sunlight coming down through leaves on the elm branches. Is the dazzle off the leaves or off the sunlight?

562. So, we treat our ideas, our practices, our understandings now, as if we had won the election, and were settled in office. While the Past, it seems, though being ineligible to vote, lost the election so can no longer form a government. But this is a democracy, so shouldn't they too have a vote? Isn't there absentee voting? And if the postal votes were to be counted, couldn't they still muster the numbers to win the election in a landslide? And I haven't mentioned the Future. But then they *will* have the vote, won't they (and we won't).

562 *int.* Your understanding of yourself is a durable platitude in sentences you no longer bother to comprehend or remember.

563. Lone bird on a telegraph wire hunching its back and puffing the feathers out to keep warm in a cold wind.

564. I guess we need to make a living, even as poets/intellectuals. But we have an obligation to keep accounts here—and have them publicly

audited. Truth, at *some* level, is obligatory in our game; and in this era truth, very clearly stated, about the sources of income and the possibility of suborning of evidence is one sort of bottom line.

565. While I don't believe in "things as they are", I sometimes believe in things-as-they-are-not. I believe that thought systems can get themselves into a tangle, wanting to go in different directions at the same time, and trip themselves up. And you don't want to stick a foot out, but you don't need to tell someone his shoelace is undone either.

566. Hunger? When I was younger and fitter, the body would tell me how much food I needed, and what. Not that I always listened to it.

567. Life's as awkward sometimes as sneezing while you're having a piss.

568. You move out—though not into air but into the light: the sun clinging dazzlingly to the trees. Green nature strips the only thing still absorbing not reflecting it, giving your eye a rest.

569. On the road, on the footpath, jostling to the front in queues—"at your inconvenience"—to shove the old politenesses aside in the new freedom—liberation from those old stifling conventions—or in fact, from having to think about people at all.

570. The jet aeroplane landing you at another place too soon. Your mind, your heart need take time to make the journey on foot and meet up with you there, so that the whole of you can get yourselves tentatively together again.

571. Ownership of the world? I don't think we own anything, at base—even our own bodies, the whole of which change every seven years or so. We're tenants of various worlds though, yet I don't feel I'm even a tenant of Australia now. It's like nobody's realized my lease has been terminated.

572. The misfortunes of our friends give us a chance to practise our sympathy and assistance. To convince them that we *are* still their friends—and to convince ourselves.

573. "On your toes!" in somebody else's shoes.

574. "Nude men in sculpture are not as beautiful as toads." (Brancusi)

575. For every young kid, events are a drama—on opening night. They "pluck the day" like there's no other, with all the intensity of what's never to be repeated. But *we* know we're in for a long season, with matinée sessions and more rehearsals. There's always next night's performance, so we may as well relax and take it as it comes—to conserve our energy and get through to the end of the season. While there'll always be another one next year.

576. Whithered dreams?

577. I have some fear of death, but more of not having done what was there for me to do in life. And a Last Judgment carried out by myself on myself, to give me the thumbs down in my own self-constructed colosseum pit.

578. Some speculative dreamers live not so much in the indicative mood where they are, but in the subjunctive mood where they might have been.

579. Sexton, in earlier days, digging up clods with shovel, tossing them up out, digging further, before lowering coffin into the grave on ropes with his assistants. A relative scatters a handful of earth and a red rose onto the coffin lid. Then after the service, the sexton returns to commence shovelling the clods back into the grave and onto the coffin.

580. The whole of friendship is shot through with evanescence—friendship and acquaintanceship leading into and away from each other—not to say our relationship with ourselves, and to the whole of life—brief, fleeting, and curling like fog in and out from everything and everyone else.

581. Your position on the summit of a mountain is like that of an ant, but also like one of the Gods—or a human being as small as the people you see at the foot of the mountain, while, unlike the Gods, looking down as much on yourself as others. But the winds ruffle the stillness and bring change, even if the mountains and valley remain changeless. Vastness and unity across stillness in motion.

582. "Time wounds all heels." (Groucho Marx)

583. Achilles had a tendency to get himself into trouble.

583 *int*. You're where you are not where you might have been. Though it's often not clear where you are, but seems very clear where you might have been.

584.

585. Catching a train back from Ellura and Ajanta. When I arrived again at the station the train was, to my astonishment, about to depart on time. I clambered quickly aboard, but couldn't find my sleeping compartment. I was dog-tired—I hadn't slept for the last two nights—and the travellers in the (2nd or) 3rd class carriage I wandered into kindly made room for me on the luggage racks so I could sleep there. But it *wasn't* on time. It was in fact the train scheduled two trains before, and fully four hours late. The locals wouldn't have normally turned up until three hours after it had been scheduled to depart. Here, punctuality itself was only at a remove—and I had to adjust my watch to their loitering conception of time.

586. Abstractions usually have their time spans attached to them—think of the 18th century's "sublime". The ostensibly more enduring ones, like "essence", have more than once changed their meanings without notice, usually dragging the echoes of the earlier meanings along in their wake. They can also change into their opposites—so that "essence" and "substance" become interchangeable.

587. Some puns are so funny because they're so bad. Mediocre isn't good/ bad enough for their effect. They have to be appalling. Similarly, some humour is so funny because it's rank. We're astonished that the comedian isn't ashamed at the garbage he's prompting us to laugh at. And the laughter is sometimes just at him or, in the depths, at the idiots in us all.

588. "Livingdying is extraordinary, but is anything ordinary? What isn't unique?" (Corman) Well, if this is so, *being unique itself*, isn't unique.

588 *int*. Beware of ideas with too snug a fit.

589. A smudge of light reflected from the curve of the shoulder bone.

590. "The end we reach isn't the end of much." (Bronk)

591. We don't have intuitions all the time, possibly because we're normally too busy to allow them to make an appearance. Whatever, they are irregular visitors, and certainly are not punctual for the major events. And perhaps would not be so, even if we were more attentive to the possibility of their occasional visits.

592. A bit woozy today. Hope it's some small time virus that doesn't like me enough to keep hanging around till it's really gotten to know me.

593. A red sun settles on the ocean's horizon, bulging squat before slipping down.

594. Put out the hand to feel if rain's falling—and the weight of it, if it is.

594 *int*. Eternal Living? I'd have a problem with the *identity* of the me that had kept itself living for ever, lingering on past its great-great-grandchildren as an "individual", necessarily adrift of anything in time and space that could make it specific.

595. Ocean, with creeks of air running off it.

596. The term "God"—the one without definite or indefinite article, and used like a personal name—is a package which ties up many incompatible things, but has reached its use-by date. We should sort through the package and select out anything that religiously is still of some use, not approach it like an individual person with only the single name, that we shouldn't be rude to, but should treat with overawed respect just in case He happens to exist. (Pascal's wager)

597. At the age when some women start calling you "dear" and "darling', who don't call *everybody* "dear" and "darling". I've been a bit bemused by it, as I'm not the "dear" or "darling" sort. But perhaps they just see I'm quiet and not cantankerous, so the rote view can kick in. I don't know if there's fire left in me still, but there's a heck of a lot of brimstone.

598. The "Subjectivity/Objectivity" axis is reinforced by the sort of solipsism that eventuates from Descartes' Cogito, and its almost parodic logical developments by Berkeley (an Irishman) and Hume (a Scot)— and then its settling in as psychological isolation in the more modern psyche. It's almost like a door's been locked in the middle of what before had been just open air.

599. White spindrift under grey cloud—the wave, the cloud rolling over at different pacings.

600. But the "I" that finally dies is a very reduced "I", granted there is such a thing, and a very changed one—not just in itself but in its setting— which is a great part of what had constituted it. Most of the people it's known, gone. Most of the places it's known, changed from when it lived there. And the residue of itself in the present but off the scene, arriving unexpectedly at the synchronised time for its last disappearance, is hardly of enough substance to be noticed departing.

601. The relationship ends abruptly, yet you are still, you think, in negotiations with the other party, but there's no reciprocal response. You're left on a stage by yourself, footlights and spotlight unswitched off; but the other actors are performing at a rival theatre, and the audience has vacated not just the auditorium but the foyer, and are unlikely to return for the next act. Still, there's not going to be one.

602. Cloud shadows moving across shallow water like seaweed under a pier.

603. It's not that you want to *win*, in most arguments, it's that you don't want to lose. A mutually accepted draw is fine, but extremely difficult to negotiate.

604. Yes, we *can* shift "community opinion" by blurring the boundaries, so that, for example, patting bottoms becomes a form of rape. And for a while "rape" will still mean rape, too. After that, though, the fudging of boundaries will be complete, and rape itself will seem very much more like the patting of bottoms than it could ever have seemed before—so the edge in the public's mind would have been blunted. This is the advertiser's trick—and the Community Advertiser's trick—to gain a competitive

edge. But it only lasts for a time, and after the boundaries have been finally blurred, the language will have been contaminated permanently and—apart from anything else—will no longer again be manipulable for this particular sophistry.

605. The actors in my life have for the most part been performing at a rival theatre.

606. Dark knot in the wood of the half-log's stopped the axe head as both've clunked onto the chopping block.

607. Us oldies often deal in out-of-date flippancy—which the young recognize as flippancy, though they're not in touch with the humour. Better, no doubt, than the weight of accrued experience we *could* dump onto them—and on ourselves.

608. The aerated drink sprinkling spray onto you over the top of the glass.

609. Blooding the tyro fox hunter at the site of the first kill. There's enough death around without bloody well being blooded into it.

610. You'll get reactions, finally, against the cultural hegemony of any particular time, but they'll never swing back to the older contrary positions that the present had originally reacted against—even when the restorators want them to do exactly that—but to newer contrary positions usually without the older contrary positions in mind, but generated from contemporary reactions against now. So, the Romantics wanted to return to the Middle Ages (as they understood them), but never looked like arriving anywhere in the vicinity. And the Middle Ages they dreamt up were both highly imaginative and unimaginable.

While classical music lovers wish to return to music at the time of Beethoven and Brahms, but (unknowingly) without the forces that were driving music, and even these composers, towards a later atonality. If you successfully retreat to a past it will most likely develop as that past *did* develop and eventuate in the present—as our future.

But this normally won't happen, and the development will be off to somewhere else.

611. And what does Rudd think of Bush? He was a diplomat—so not only wouldn't he say it, he wouldn't think it either. But there's no doubt what he wouldn't think.*

* *This diplomatic tactfulness was in fact shattered when Rudd rang Bush to discuss some matter to be raised at a G20 meeting they were both to attend ten days on. Bush then enquired "What's the G20?" Now Rudd was a mite surprised by this as Bush was meant not merely to be attending this meeting but to be chairing it.*

612. Contemporary life tries to exorcise despair as "pessimism"—while it's moral to be "optimistic"; yet it's easily the most despairing age I've seen, and been reluctant fellow-traveller in. And I believe that shunning mention of and knowledge of reality puts fear of what it might be rather than knowledge of what it is, in place; and fears of being unable to cope with it, too. You only find out what you can cope with *in the event*, not by anxietising about what it allegedly might be, in anticipation.

613. Summer flapping in early like a loose flock of magpies.

Midsummer hopping in, in jerks, like a plague of locusts, tossed-up and re-tossed up in spasms and jerky flights.

Summer-to-autumn, winging in like a tight swarm of gnats.

614. A smug modesty.

615. Would newer acquaintances appreciate us better than long term friends? Only while we'd still be a mutual novelty, and hadn't sized each other up or down.

(Corollary to La Roche)

616. Our dominant virtue usually has its correlative vice along with it as a constant companion. For example, an easygoing accommodation to events and to people will degenerate into sloth as its habitual consequence, having kept company with it for most of its life, or the energetic organizer will develop into a manipulative prick or bitch, no longer able to quickly get its way.

617. "The weight of spiritless years." (Tsvetayeva)

618. Freedom should properly be *from* something, and thus a negative (though powerful), rather than a substantive in its own right. Whereas the big ideal, with a capital F and airwaves of rhetoric behind it, still only erects its banner when people are freed *from* something—an invader, class distinction, discrimination, poverty, oppression.

619. White summer sun in and out of a storm sky, mopping up and unmopping up an eerie radiance.

620. A dear elder friend of mine from the past, Trevor Artingstall, when I was complaining of foul treatment by people we both knew, would reply "But Clive, they're just children". And this was hard to take, and still is, because they were a decade or two older than me, and had done nasty things from positions of authority. But there's a lot of just-childenry around, and it's unfortunately necessary, when becoming an adult, to learn to treat even your elders like children, both positively and negatively. I didn't quite learn the religious empathy for them that Trevor was beckoning to—it's a test of one's saintliness that I was always likely to fail, and am still not certain I should have attempted to succeed at.

620 *int*. We have a method of isolating our facts one by one, halting at one fact, then another, to settle each one distinctly down, before we re-imagine this discontinuity as a continuity.

621. Bamboo branches mixing their leaves in and out through the breeze.

622. Christ: "I will come like a thief in the night". More like robbery with violence than just stealing—wouldn't you think?

623. Beliefs are of the nature of presuppositions, and are cornerstones of structures of understanding that would not stay erect without the beliefs. Some of these structures should have a demolition job done on them, and it is one of the thinker's tasks to examine any presupposition for instability. But it is nobody else's task, and anyone pursuing it has got a duty not to be selective in the pursuit. Anyone else not a thinker will come up with reinforcements of some sector of their own culture's presuppositions/ prejudices, and an aversion to those of others—with, that is to say, their

own culture's / subculture's platitudes or ur-platitudes—and there can be quite a lot of instability in those.

624. Early, still cool on a summer's morning. The ocean flat enough to stretch out, and the far-away-from-land still coupled to here.

625. So when he wrote: "The idea of God makes no sense to me whatsoever", I realized that the Vienna Circle's tendentious identification of meaning and verifiability had degraded down into the educated populace's moves to brand thinking from outside their prejudices as "nonsense".

626. Cow moving tail with jaw. Keeps eye on us to check whether distance far enough off to maintain its tranquillity.

627. One of the reasons we regret the passing of our friends is because of the inconclusiveness of our relationships with them, and the sense of lost opportunity either to cement the relationships or break them that had still been available to us back then.

628. I always wondered how Esther Williams and chorus avoided swallowing or inhaling water into those big cheesy grins, while they were commencing their submersions.

629. There's both positive and negative luck. The second when you manage to avoid disasters, potential or actual—as an aeroplane crash when you were meant to be on the plane. The first when you win the lottery. Superstitiously, when I've received positive luck, I've always felt the Fates were ready to unbalance me and balance the books—to even things up.

630. The lake/pond surface, with reeds to one side: some places rough, some places smooth; but rough and smooth patches stable in their own areas—under a light wind.

631. Into that time of life when you get only repetition—or memories of events that were in fact never to be repeated.

632. The wind flattens shine across the poplars.

633. I pointed out that the negative thing about hypocrisy—when a gap has been accepted between principle and practice—was not just that people did not have to practise what they preached, but that they could espouse principles they did not have at all; and that if there were enough of these people, and in the right places, principles themselves would come to be considered merely as rhetorical instruments to manipulate the gullibility of the audience or the electorate, and to be taken as cynically as a mountebank's sales pitch. And later, that the very idea of principles would become obsolete.

634. The avenue of plane trees splashes sunlight about on it, soundlessly, off gold leaves and brown.

634 *int*. Moral rules, with "Community Advertising", have been reduced to commercial slogans, memorable for a time.

635. I don't know what all this subtracts down to.

636. We scraped the carrots then diced them, peeled spuds then split them. Slipped spinach, for greens, into the stew.

637. I'm usually trying to understand; or to understand what I don't understand; or to understand in what *way* I don't understand. I have given it all up, at times, temporarily. But I don't think there's an *overall* to understand—as all understandings, for me, are in the plural, and are connected to particular places / times. My more general conclusions would be, roughly, Proustian—that categories (especially visual) filter out direct memories of what we've experienced before, and standardize them into just the categories themselves.

So what we learn, when we "learn from experience", is frequently what we've been all too ready to learn, using the terms set down for us, and not straying from any preordained presuppositions.

638. The young are addicts for love and sex, but time teaches them how to break the habit. Not that everyone will learn the lesson.

639. Nations of *identical individuals*, as a concept, doesn't seem as risible as it should seem. As Kant might have indicated, "individual" is not a predicate. There's no *quality* needed to be one, just a single digit number.

640. Why do events seem emptier in age? Because of the repetition? You've seen this before, or something very like it, and you collect and catalogue it again, adding to the number of similar incidents you have on record, and giving more gravity to the weight of your generalisations from them. But only once have you seen it fresh—that was when you first came across it many years ago. Now you look not so much at the particular event but at its generic type, and slot it away in its correct file, without repeating any more that direct contact you'd once had with it.

641. The shovelled earth, packed and adhering to roots weighted down with it.

642. A half-spiral tower of children's colour blocks stretching teeteringly off the carpet.

643. Space missions? It's like sending men off for a far-flung explanation, to gravitate the planets and the stars.

644 "…feeling … a sense of space—since your lady is away?'" Probably, as a bit of a nonentity, unconnected with the world. A lot of other people in that plight, so I'd better get used to it. And stop not just my whingeing, but the pre-whingeing leading up to it.

645. Slim girls with round breasts—heavy peaches on slender branches.

646. The Romantic movement elevated ordinary social impulses into something more transcendent—like forces of nature, storms or the sea, raging within the diminutive breasts.

647. "Death. Mortality. For me it is the crux of life…" (Cid Corman) Certainly. Apart from anything else, because death and life are the only contraries for each other. And among the few contraries that, while they can only be understood in relation to each other—as would be all contraries—are also in some sense absolutes. They're important concepts— and we puzzle about them a lot. And ought to, for that matter—it's the human thing to do, at depth. And we brood on the losses. "The world was my oyster" when young. I don't think it's anybody's oyster now—but certainly not mine. And it's not my world anyhow. *My* world had my brother in it, and mother and father, and best friend. And yes, a couple

of places in Melbourne where I saw my brother on his visits there in his last years, would still be my world—I could still do some living there, preferably in the company of all of us.

648. A lot of good-and-evil, and beyond-good-and-evil in Dostoyevsky. I'm not sure where I am with that any more; nor with the passion (in the Latin sense of the term) nor the kenosis, nor the abasement. Nor whether heaven and hell have the grandeur and degradation needed for the throes of the Dostoyevskian character. Does such a creation need something deep-darker or more ecstatic for both interim and final ends?

649.

650. To look upon the stars as dead planets—bright, always without an audience. Yes I know they're really suns—if you stared at them long enough, would they burn your eyes out?

651. Across the beach, ripples in sand shaped to the tide's retreating waters.

652. The question of the will to understanding, and why one wants to keep on doing anything as a poet, when it's neither the body nor the social animal insisting on its needs—and where nobody's particularly asked you to do it, nor cares much whether you do it or don't.

653. The wash of low tide—transparent shallowness showing currents and ripple.

654. "Things are getting worse." "Oh, but that's what people have always said." "Why shouldn't this be evidence that it's true? I bet if people had always said 'things are getting better', it *would* be taken as evidence that that particular proposition was true."

655. The established intellectuals and literary men are not looking for equals, in people new on the scene, but for younger disciples. Like parrots to have on their shoulders—each parrot with its patch over one eye.

655 *int.* Music has to be performed in time, and is a temporal event; yet the manuscript form has been already completed, so is outside of time, or

at least the time of any performance of it: a sort of theoretical impossibility, solved in practice, like a zen koan, by the act of the performance.

656.

657. Pylons suspend the power lines, straddling abstract across paddocks.

657 *int*. The Miroku-bosatsu at Koryuji. Easy to photograph the image of a statue, from one angle; but not the space around it, or within it, nor how you move around that space and the statue moves motionless with you and the space.

658. "Wish my brothers could share the poems … but that's the size of things isn't it?" (Cid Corman) I meant to show Owen (brother) my work but after mum died—as I couldn't afford any poems about her to be used tactically in the war that would frequently break out between them. And I could trust him not to be trusted on *that* score—though he was completely trustworthy on others. And then he died before she did, and he never got to see them. Cid's ones, with so many shared experiences, environs and the like—would've been, almost, meant for his brothers; but the poems eventuated after their deaths. Life doesn't time itself, often, to the quick or slow march of our plans.

659. No, No—I don't want to be "resurrected", reincarnated or metem-psychosed. Besides, it's not possible: it'd be somebody else—or, more accurately, another congeries of physical and psychic traits. Mind you, this here collection of physical and psychic traits, after dispersal, will get themselves into various other congeries, and one or two traits might even renew acquaintance over the millennia—if we *have* any more millennia.

660. I moved away from Mozart and Bach, a little, when it seemed I might have worn out my welcome with them, and we might no longer have understood each other so well. It'd become like perpetually listening to the one recorded message.

661. As my friend Trevor Artingstall pointed out all those years ago, the Indians regularly use sedatives, like betel juice—spitting out long red squirts of it all over the ground—while we Westerners need stimulants, so we can "have an edge", and find whatever empty life we have as

"exciting". And where does all this excitement get you? Well, in fact, stimulants, taken in sufficient quantity, become depressants.

662. The blue, opening between clouds. Closing. Reopening.

663. What do "Think of every day as special, as if it were your last" and "There's nothing special about any day" have in common? They both treat life as if it had one pace—with no ebbs and flows.

664. We carry people's memories like a face in a locket. You flick open the lid, underneath you flick open the face.

665. After you're gone, you sometimes leave your smudge around for a time.

666. Much of the "grandeur" in art is misplaced military glory—and from the victorious whatsmore, after decimating the enemy's army. Something central in our art. Even the tenderness, even peace, get some of their power in positive or negative relation to this annihilating grandeur.

667. Whatever else, one learns that the accepted sense of time and progression being as constant as a clock is not how life enacts itself. It speeds up, slows down, has stoppings in fits and starts—and can be unexpected as to how it changes its pace, and when.

668. "…is Cid (in a coma) getting bored exploring that nether world of Livingdying he's been in…?" (Chuck Sandy). Probably. I see a lot of life as being lived in that nether world anyhow, and we only sharpen or blunten our assumptions about it—as being clear as daylight, or opaque as a burial ground—for practical purposes, and to feel secure (though it doesn't mean anyone will actually *be* secure).

668 *int.* I have a better sense of what my father *didn't* say to me now, than I did have—though I always had some sense of it.

669. This shadow will never be here again—stretched out by a late afternoon sun into nearly three times its length—and never the same group of spectators, nor the squatting batsman attempting to flick another leg glance off, before being out leg-before, with the appeal of all fieldsmen turning into a shout for joy.

Earlier times would have fixed this transience by thinking of the continuity of the setting suns, or of cricket matches being repeated into eternity, or thinking that the prototypes were eternal, so that the repeated instances were of as little importance as each other, but significant because of the types.

Yet modern times want to "live for the day" in a new sense, and inhabit the moment—not times past and times future. This is something like the mystic's moment, but concentrates more on pleasure and on activity—though sometimes on the "still moment" near the heart—and uses this to obviate the sense of transience in life.

670. The pine forest, so clear, so blue-green nearer the light just under the horizon, clarifying its own shadow.

671. Growing sense of emptiness, against the grain, which used to be a positive, but's now a negative. And I'm affected by some of my friends' hope-lessness too, when I'm not natively the hopeless sort—though I know the site well enough. It's affected my sense of *their* transitoriness, their non-substantiality. (Yet again, this used to be a sort of freedom, as I saw it—like space in which to move. I don't see too much freedom in it now—like space with no boundaries to it, nothinglessness throughout. And it doesn't matter "where" you move in it.)

671 *int.* You sometimes see the look on the face of a woman in a new relationship of someone who is learning the ropes. Not on men's faces, who are not learning the ropes. Though sometimes, he has the diffidence of a person who cannot learn the ropes, and despairs of ever being able to do so.

671 *int.* "He's a deep thinker" is no longer a compliment that's current. For all our thoughts surface from the shallows of the subconscious, or are fitted together like pieces of a jigsaw.

672. "Mind/brain... schism with body." (Corman) Theoretically endorsed by Descartes, and then entrenched with new customs and gadgetry/machines—but endemic (in thought) with us since the Scholastics. The identification, at a formal level, of mind and brain is a preposterous development this century (obviously the *brain* is not in schism with the body—they work pretty well together). Actually, the

way we've conceptualized it, we *must* have "the body" and "the mind" separate—they are effectively defined against each other. To ask then how they could possibly relate is ridiculous—for they relate both closely and at a distance, in their union as the polar opposites to each other.

673. I begin to feel that I have given too little weight to the living realities, and the people, that have come in and out of my life. I've not seen anybody able to ground the passing of time however, and of worlds and of people; yet for the first time consider their distress and unbalance might be more appropriate than my own facile poise (or deep poise if I were able to maintain it in a balance), however unfacile its genesis and its justifications might have been.

674. Further out from the lap of the waves, a quiet awake on the sea.

675. "The sun and moon and earth and all its untouched (by us) components are extraordinary EVENTS and they don't cost a penny." (Cid Corman) Instantaneously, someone with a cash register heart and a double-entry bookkeeping mind will have heard this on the airwaves as a new and "exciting" opportunity. So in future people will need a license to look up at the stars.

676. "To live in the dark, to do in the dark what we can." (G. Benn)

676 *int.* "Love"—a word regularly applied to mothers, babies, one's sex partner, close friends of women, and even fathers, to ice cream and to the open air. It stretches and cramps to fit all sizes like the elastic band on underwear, and makes the world go round—or whatever shape it is. And is the cause of joy and depression—and in most cases, of confusion.

677. The reason we can treat the death of our friends so casually is because we treated them alive, so casually.

678. Rain on the hills, cloud fringe smudging into the valleys—grey mountain wall behind.

679. Christianity is a dramatic religion. Any "peace" in it would be just a short interlude in a war zone, or the "rest" in a corner, at the bell, between rounds of a prizefight, or the post-orgasmic slumber after the

turbulent attraction and repulsion that throws passionate lovers apart and together.

680. Candle flame, duplicated in the reflection on the table, from below dull depths with shiny surfaces.

681. The Requiem Mass. The rituals *do* help—though I'm not sure in what way. There was a scatter of people from many places, and from many eras in the congregation; but nobody, I think, from the contemporary parish, in what had always been our parish church. We came out of many different lives to get there, genuflected, and have now gone back into those lives, or to whatever there might be, never to return.

682. Rain on grass, droop-lengths beaten down, a last flurry still on them.

683. Drops of rain bouncing everywhere off the road.

684. "And lacks the demention of time." One thinks of Goya's Saturn Devouring his Children. It's a dimension we don't handle all that well.

685. Two dogs roll over in mock-up fight—then halt, to search for fleas in each other's hair, on each other's skin.

686. Many similarities between our relationships to our grandmothers— you and I—even though it seems they were very different characters. I tend to have two desolate thoughts about it all. First, how few people have a memory of her now, and how partial any such memory would be. Secondly, I have *no* memory of my great grandparents (nor, indeed, of one of my two grandfathers), so nothing remains in memory of them at all, anywhere. And this will shortly be true of my own grandparents. And so on. And as for memories of others? They might as well never have lived.

686 *int*. An autumn of clear light and balance, when things seem to be in stasis for a brief never-ending, and can be contemplated almost as if there will never be change—based on a feeling that change is very imminent.

687.

688. "Everything will be forgotten in the days to come." But only if there *are* days to come. And if there are no days to come, will everything still be forgotten?

www.ingramcontent.com/pod-product-compliance
Lightning Source LLC
Chambersburg PA
CBHW030339020726
47493CB00004B/1336